Planning, Connecting, and Financing Cities—Now

Urbanization Policy Framework

Plan

- **VALUE** land use through transparent assessment

- **COORDINATE** land use with infrastructure, natural resources, and hazard risk

- **LEVERAGE** competitive markets alongside regulation to expand basic services

Connect

- **VALUE** the city's external and internal connections

- **COORDINATE** among transport options and with land use

- **LEVERAGE** investments that will generate the largest returns— individually and collectively

Finance

- **VALUE** and develop the city's creditworthiness

- **COORDINATE** public-private finance using clear, consistent rules

- **LEVERAGE** existing assets to develop new ones, and link both to land use planning

Helping City Leaders Address Key Challenges

Improving living conditions, especially in slums	Managing the city's physical form	Creating jobs	Expanding the coverage and quality of basic infrastructure services	Bridging the divided city and fostering inclusion

Planning, Connecting, and Financing Cities—Now

Priorities for City Leaders

THE WORLD BANK
Washington, DC

Contents

BOXES

FIGURES

MAPS

TABLES

Foreword

Cities are where development challenges and solutions meet. With the cities of emerging economies expected to double from 2 billion to 4 billion people between 2000 and 2030—accompanied by a tripling of their physical footprint from 200,000 to 600,000 square kilometers—the policies and investments that get this rapid urbanization right hold the key to resilient and sustainable development. The good news is that cities in the developing world can build on the knowledge of those that have been successful before them and combine these insights with homegrown solutions and innovations to catalyze the engines of job creation, centers of innovation, and gateways to the global marketplace.

To help mayors and other policy makers identify the bottlenecks they face as urbanization accelerates and to propose policy options to tackle such challenges, the World Bank—with support from the Swiss State Secretariat for Economic Affairs (SECO) and the Cities Alliance—has carried out diagnostics called "Urbanization Reviews" in 12 countries across 4 continents. This program has created a bedrock of credible facts and a set of solutions that are tailored to the fiscal, political, and administrative realities of cities.

This book, *Planning, Connecting, and Financing Cities—Now* distills the lessons learned from these diagnostics into a practical framework for sustainable urbanization, which is organized around the three policy pillars of the title. The coordination among these pillars is critical, particularly the relationship between land use planning and hazard risk, housing, infrastructure, and urban transport. This framework has already helped to reshape core urbanization policy debates and to integrate action across the urban space in countries such as Colombia, India, Uganda, and Vietnam. For example, In India, the Urbanization Review provided considerable inputs to the teams that shaped the contours of the 12th Five-Year Plan; in Colombia, the Urbanization Review helped in the design of a Mission for Cities—the product of a high-level committee for urban management.

We encourage you to read this report, and that you look at your own city and assess its planning, connecting, and financing and how they are coordinated to support sustainable urbanization.

Zoubida Allaoua
Director, Urban and Disaster Risk
Management Department, World Bank

Beatrice Maser Mallor, Head of Economic
Cooperation and Development, Swiss State
Secretariat for Economic Affairs (SECO)

Marianne Fay
Chief Economist, Sustainable
Development Network, World Bank

William Cobbett
Program Manager, Cities Alliance

Acknowledgments

This report was written by a team led by Somik V. Lall and composed of Om Prakash Agarwal, David Dowall, Michael Klein, Nancy Lozano-Gracia, and Hyoung Gun Wang. Significant contributions were made by Isabel Chatterton, Michael Jacobsen, Henry Jewell, Austin Kilroy, Andreas Kopp, Dennis Linders, Lili Liu, Chris Rodrigo, Eugenia Suarez, Hiroaki Suzuki, Nozomi Tokiwa, Sarah Elizabeth Antos, and Katie L. McWilliams. Tara Vishwanath acted as adviser to the Urbanization Review program. The team thanks Indermit Gill for his time, advice, and guidance on sharpening the policy framework used in this report. Berenice Sanchez Suarez and Fernando Armendaris provided outstanding support.

This report draws on Urbanization Review prototypes that seek to build a body of knowledge on urbanization challenges and public policy implications in a variety of country settings. These prototypes have been piloted in Brazil, China, Colombia, India, Indonesia, the Republic of Korea, Sri Lanka, Tunisia, Turkey, Uganda, and Vietnam. We are grateful to Dean Cira, Peter Ellis, Steve Karam, Taimur Samad, Rachel Sebudde, and Tara Vishwanath for leading these country pilots.

The policy framework of this report has benefited from discussions with Junaid Ahmed, Bianca Baerlocher, Jose Alejandro Bayona, Eric Berg, Alain Bertaud, Marlon Boarnet, Jan Brueckner, Julia Bucknall, Dean Cira, Uwe Deichmann, Jean Jacques Dethier, Michelle Gysin, Stéphane Hallegatte, Sonia Hammam, Vernon Henderson, Geoffrey Hewings, Markus Huber, Jin-Cheol Jo, Matthew Kahn, Steve Karam, Christine Kessides, Andreas Kopp, David Kramer, Won-yong Kwon, Dag Larsson, Lili Liu, Om Prakash Mathur, Rakesh Mohan, Stefano Negri, Jae-Gil Park, Sam Ock Park, Yang-Ho Park, Jose Antonio Pinzon, Juan Mauricio Ramirez, L. Nicolas Ronderos, Tony Venables, and Robert D. Yaro. We appreciate the opportunity to discuss the policy framework and findings at various forums including the Cities Alliance Consultative Group Meetings (Maputo), Center for Mediterranean Integration (Marseilles), Center for Policy Research (New Delhi), Departamento Nacional De Planeacion (Bogotá), Global Energy Basel Summit (Basel), Swiss State Secretariat for Economic Affairs workshop (Berne), Korea Research Institute for Human Settlements (Seoul), Ministerio de Desarrollo Urbano y Vivienda (Quito), Norway Ministry of Foreign Affairs (Oslo), Planning Commission of India (New Delhi),Toulouse School of Economics (Toulouse), University of Illinois (Urbana-Champaign), and the World Bank (Washington, DC).

This report was sponsored by the Sustainable Development Network of the World Bank. Financial support for the Urbanization

Reviews was provided by the Cities Alliance and the Swiss State Secretariat for Economic Affairs (SECO). The report has been produced under the supervision of Abha Joshi Ghani, practice head for Urban Development, and the overall direction of Zoubida Allaoua, Director of the Urban and Disaster Risk Management Department, and Marianne Fay, Chief Economist of the Sustainable Development Network. Nick Moschovakis and Bruce Ross-Larson, with a team that included Rob Elson and Jack Harlow at Communications Development Inc., edited the report.

About the Authors

Somik V. Lall is a Lead Economist for Urban Development at the World Bank's Disaster Risk and Urban Management Department. He was a core team member of the *World Development Report 2009: Reshaping Economic Geography,* and recently Senior Economic Counselor to the Indian Prime Minister's National Transport Development Policy Committee. He currently leads a World Bank program on the Urbanization Reviews, which provides diagnostic tools and a policy framework for policy makers to manage rapid urbanization and city development. His research interests span urban and spatial economics, infrastructure development, and public finance, with more than 40 publications featured in peer-reviewed journals, edited volumes, and working papers. He holds a bachelor's degree in engineering, a master's in city planning, and a doctorate in economics and public policy.

Nancy Lozano-Gracia is an economist at the World Bank who has worked extensively in the field of economic valuation of urban amenities, such as water, sanitation, and sewerage, as well as goods that are not traded in the market (such as air quality). She is a core team member of the Urbanization Reviews effort at the World Bank, and her work has covered Brazil, Colombia, India, Turkey, and Vietnam. She holds a doctorate in applied economics from the University of Illinois.

O.P. Agarwal has been working at the World Bank's Transport Anchor since 2009. He leads a World Bank team that has designed and is delivering a Capacity Building program for Leaders in Urban Transport Planning. He has been a member of the Indian Administrative Service (IAS), the premier civil service in India. He held several positions, both under the national government and under the provincial government. He has written several papers on urban transport policy and governance issues. He has a bachelor's degree in electrical engineering from the Indian Institute of Technology, Chennai; a master's degree in transportation from the Massachusetts Institute of Technology, Cambridge, USA; and a doctorate from the Indian Institute of Technology, Delhi.

David Dowall has worked for the World Bank for the past 27 years, designing urban development projects in more than 200 cities in nearly 50 countries. He was a professor of city and regional planning at the University of California at Berkeley from 1976 to 2012. His professional and research work spans strategic and spatial planning, economic development, infrastructure planning, and finance. He has published more than 100 books, academic journal articles, and professional reports. He has a bachelor's degree in economics from the University of Maryland, a master's in urban and regional planning from the University of Colorado, and a doctorate in economics also from the University of Colorado.

Michael Klein is Professor at the Frankfurt School of Finance and Management in Germany and a Senior Adjunct Professor at the School of Advanced International Studies of Johns Hopkins University. Michael worked at the World Bank (1982–2009), most recently as Vice President for Financial and Private Sector Development for the World Bank Group as well as Chief Economist, International Finance Corporation. He was Chief Economist of the Royal Dutch/Shell Group (1997–2000) and headed the unit for non-OECD economies at the OECD Economics Department (1991–93). Michael studied in Bonn, New Haven, and Paris and received his doctorate in economics from Bonn University, Germany.

Hyoung Gun Wang is an economist in the Disaster Risk and Urbanization Management Department of the World Bank. He is a core team member of the Urbanization Review flagship study of the World Bank. His research interests are urbanization and urban development, urban and regional economics, spatial economic analysis, economic impacts of infrastructure investment, disaster management methodology, and economic growth at the regional and local levels. His research and work programs have spanned a range of developing countries including Brazil, China, the Democratic Republic of Congo, the Russian Federation, Turkey, and Vietnam, among others. He holds a doctorate in economics from Brown University.

Abbreviations

BOT	Build, operate, and transfer
BRT	Bus rapid transit
FAR	Floor area ratio
FINDETER	Financiera de Desarrollo Territorial (Colombia)
FSI	Floor space index
GDP	Gross domestic product
GRDP	Gross regional domestic product
ICT	Information and communication technology
IDU	Instituto de Desarrollo Urbano, Urban Development Institute (Colombia)
NEN	National Expressway Network (China)
NWSC	National Water and Sewerage Corporation (Uganda)
OECD	Organisation for Economic Co-operation and Development
PLN	Perusahaan Listrik Negara, state electricity company (Indonesia)
PMIB	Programa de Mejoramiento Integral de Barrios (Colombia)
PPP	Public-private partnership
SAR	Special administrative region
SEZ	Special economic zone
TNUDF	Tamil Nadu Urban Development Fund (India)
VT	*Vale transporte,* transportation vouchers (Brazil)

*All monetary values are in U.S. dollars unless otherwise noted.

Overview

The world's first cities were in the Uruk Cluster in Mesopotamia. The largest was Ur, which appears in the Epic of Gilgamesh (one of the earliest known works of literature, set around 3,500 BCE). Extending over 60 hectares, Ur was home to about 24,000 people. But as an irrigation city—also providing marketing and defense services—it governed and extracted surpluses from a neighboring population of about 500,000. Its urban population was densely concentrated, more than 400 people per hectare, and the planning practices were strikingly sophisticated. With four main residential areas, Ur offered its inhabitants basic amenities such as well-laid-out streets and sanitation.

Cities have thus been planned from the beginning, enabling new settlements, economic specialization, and cultural expression. The growth of cities is driven largely by the economic prosperity they help create. By enabling density—the concentration of people and economic activities in a small geographic space—cities have helped transform economies for many centuries. High densities enable social and economic interactions at a much higher frequency than in nonurban settings. These interactions create a vibrant market for ideas that translates into innovations by entrepreneurs and investors. Indeed,

50 percent of world gross domestic product (GDP) is produced on just 1.5 percent of the world's land, almost all of it in cities (World Bank 2008). And various estimates point out that more than 80 percent of global GDP is generated in cities, with this share increasing rapidly.

But today, cities are growing at an unprecedented and challenging speed. City leaders are concerned about creating jobs and making their cities competitive. They also worry about the quality of life for citizens, and how cities can lower their carbon trajectories.[1] The city populations of emerging economies are expected to double between 2000 and 2030, from 2 billion to 4 billion people. Megacities, such as Tokyo, Mexico City, and São Paulo, are already home to 30 million people or more. The built-up area of cities worldwide will triple in size, from 200,000 to 600,000 square kilometers. Such rapid population growth accompanied by an even faster spatial expansion of cities may lead to low-density development dominated by individual-vehicle transportation—a largely irreversible pattern (World Bank 2012b). With more than 70 percent of generated energy now consumed in cities, and as much as 80 percent of global greenhouse gas emissions attributed to urban residents—and with vulnerability to natural

1

hazards increasingly concentrated in cities—getting this rapidly paced urbanization right is the key to resilient and sustainable growth.

This report is written for city leaders, but *city leaders* does not just mean mayors. It means anyone whose position—local, municipal, provincial, or national—gives him or her a policy- or decision-making role and thereby a stake in urban development.[2] City leaders are mayors, but they are also directors of community-based organizations; they are subnational and national policy makers and ministers (of finance, investment, and planning); and they are private sector investors, developers, and service providers.

The report provides a framework to help city leaders make informed decisions for sustainable development in their cities. What must be done to improve living conditions, especially in slums and hazard-prone areas? To create jobs? To bridge the divided cities (inclusion)? To expand the coverage and quality of basic infrastructure services? To manage the city's physical form? In trying to address these challenges, city leaders often pursue targeted investments—providing housing subsidies, increasing infrastructure spending, or creating new growth poles. Yet history shows us that a more comprehensive set of rules is needed.

To think comprehensively about how policy and investment choices can influence the pace, magnitude, and impact of urbanization and city development, the World Bank has developed a program of diagnostics called the Urbanization Reviews. These diagnostics are being carried out in collaboration with city leaders in several pilot countries (box O.1).

At the heart of the diagnostic approach used in the Urbanization Reviews are the three main dimensions of urban development (figure O.1), also the focus of the three main chapters in this report:

- *Planning*—charting a course for cities by setting the terms of urbanization, especially policies for using urban land and expanding basic infrastructure and public services.
- *Connecting*—making a city's markets (labor, goods, and services) accessible to other cities and to other neighborhoods in the city, as well as to outside export markets.
- *Financing*—finding sources for large capital outlays needed to provide infrastructure and services as cities grow and urbanization picks up speed.

And for the framework of *planning, connecting, and financing* to work, a good governance structure is a prerequisite. City leaders, at all government levels, will have to work together. If this fails, everything else will stumble.

Planning, connecting, and financing—these are terms that policy makers use on a daily basis, but they often place financing first without fully considering the other two dimensions. Of the three dimensions, *planning* for land use and basic services is primary. Yet because planning must allow for people and products to be mobile, it must be coordinated with connecting at all stages of a city's growth. What follows then is *financing*: a dimension that, although as necessary as the other two, should be city leaders' last concern rather than their first.

This point cannot be emphasized too strongly. A primary focus on financing—though understandable as an attempt to meet urgent needs—is likely to result in unplanned cities if it is not coordinated with planning and connecting. And that will lock a city into undesirable physical forms that can set back its development for decades, even centuries. A city's physical structures, once established, may remain in place for more than 150 years (Hallegatte 2009).

Putting financing first, without full consideration of the other dimensions, is a mistake because it often neglects the overriding need to coordinate infrastructure improvements (connecting) with policies (planning). And the lack of such coordination will be regretted by later urban generations. For example, in Hanoi, Vietnam, a projected new mass transit system will extend in several directions from today's central business district—but it will not reach an emerging second central business district, southwest of the city, where dense housing developments

BOX O.1   Thinking through policy and investment choices using the World Bank's Urbanization Reviews

Lessons from developed and urbanized countries can help rapidly urbanizing ones. Synthesizing such lessons was the aim of the 2009 *World Development Report: Reshaping Economic Geography* (World Bank 2008). The report looked at urbanization trends and policies worldwide, and it proposed a three-part policy framework for urbanization. First, institutions should provide the foundations for liberalizing the movement of people and goods and easing the exchange and redevelopment of land—enabling vast economic gains. Second, investments respond to the needs of residents and businesses, especially for basic and connective infrastructure. Third, targeted interventions respond to the needs of the poor and people in marginal locations or address individual behaviors that endanger health, safety, or the environment.

Applying the 2009 *World Development Report* policy framework, the World Bank's Urbanization Reviews offer city leaders diagnostic tools to identify policy distortions and analyze investment priori-

ties. Each review starts by assessing a country's or region's spatial transformation: how the urban economy is evolving, how demand for the city is changing with economic development, the pace of new arrivals, and how these new arrivals into the city are finding places to live and commuting to their jobs. It then compares the city's observed patterns with benchmarks in other places or with past conditions. Such comparisons help reveal how policy distortions constrain urbanization and how investment shortfalls restrict the benefits from it. Once the review has identified the possible constraints and shortfalls, it proposes policy options. It aims to show how a city can harness economic and social benefits not just today, but in the future, as economies grow, technologies change, and institutions are strengthened.

To test the relevance of the tools and policy framework in different development circumstances, the World Bank has piloted the Urbanization Reviews in more than 10 countries at varying stages of urbanization (see figure BO.1.1): Uganda and Sri Lanka

FIGURE BO.1.1   **Urbanization Review countries, by urbanization rate (2009) and GDP per capita (2010)**

Source: Urbanization Review team.

(where urbanization is nascent); China, India, Indonesia, and Vietnam (where it is intermediate); and Brazil, Colombia, the Republic of Korea, and Turkey (where it is mature). The reviews use one diagnostic

approach for all countries—but the policy options that are explored vary by country in their emphasis, reflecting each country's particular stage of urbanization and institutional circumstances.

(box continues on next page)

BOX O.1 (continued)

The country-specific and city-specific diagnostics of the Urbanization Reviews can identify problems and help formulate policy responses. Although the Urbanization Review is not intended to generate a policy or investment blueprint, it should help in identifying and resolving key policy distortions. In addition, because diagnostics compare present realities with what could be or should be, they imply

benchmarking—comparing performance against the situation in other places, against chosen standards, or against known best practices. The Urbanization Reviews also draw on the Banks's Urban and Local Government Strategy, "System of Cities: Harnessing Urbanization for Growth and Poverty Reduction" (World Bank 2010).

FIGURE O.1   A framework of rules: Planning, connecting, and financing

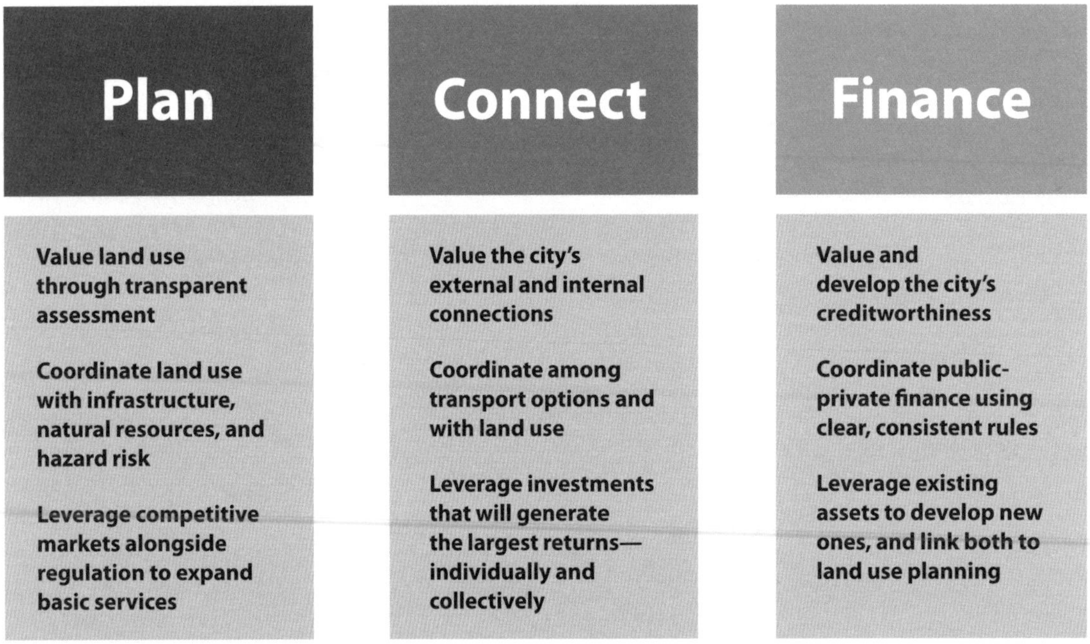

Plan	Connect	Finance
Value land use through transparent assessment	Value the city's external and internal connections	Value and develop the city's creditworthiness
Coordinate land use with infrastructure, natural resources, and hazard risk	Coordinate among transport options and with land use	Coordinate public-private finance using clear, consistent rules
Leverage competitive markets alongside regulation to expand basic services	Leverage investments that will generate the largest returns—individually and collectively	Leverage existing assets to develop new ones, and link both to land use planning

Source: Urbanization Review team.
Note: This framework draws on World Bank (2012a) and the findings from various country pilots under the Urbanization Reviews.

called New Urban Zones are already being built (map O.1).

Another example: the government of South Africa tried to save money by selecting isolated regions, with lower land values, as the sites for about 2 million newly built subsidized homes. But there was no plan to

connect these new homes to the job market. Many workers now commute in collective taxis, which are slow and expensive. The roads are not good enough to handle traffic efficiently, and several transfers are needed to reach dispersed job sites (Bertaud 2009). Buses, too, carry workers on commutes that can last nearly as long as the work day itself. Here is how a typical day passes for one South African worker:

> Jones is a limousine driver in Johannesburg . . . he lives three hours away from his place of work. He leaves home at 5:00 every morning, takes a bus and reaches his work place at 8:00. On the return, it's the same story. He leaves at 5:00 and reaches home at 8:00. On most days the only meal he is able to find time for—or even afford, due to the high travel cost—is his dinner. He sees his little daughter only on Sunday, as she is not awake by the time he leaves and is asleep by the time he gets back. (Personal communication with O. P. Agarwal, report team member)

Similarly, Colombia's urban development challenges arise from problems of policy and planning. One of Latin America's most decentralized countries, Colombia has more than 1,000 municipal governments with parallel responsibilities—basic infrastructure service delivery, land use and economic development, and social service provision. Urban areas comprise multiple municipalities: Bogotá, for example, contains seven. These municipalities lack mechanisms to coordinate policy and planning across their boundaries. As a result, Colombia's metropolitan areas are crippled by inertia—unable to coordinate their land use policies, or plan for strategic investments, at the metropolitan or regional scale that is demanded by a growing urban economy.

Also similar, Uganda's 1995 constitution created private land ownership and abolished land leases vested with local urban bodies. Local governments were fiscally starved, unable to acquire land or protect rights-of-way for infrastructure improvement. And land transactions generally were hampered by poor tenure security (only 18 percent of land is registered and titled); by the lack of a credible system for valuing land; by low incentives for landowners to rent their land; and by high entry costs for land development ventures. To remedy the situation, especially in

MAP O.1   Where financing comes first, inefficiencies are likely to follow: Uncoordinated plans for housing and mass transport in Hanoi, Vietnam

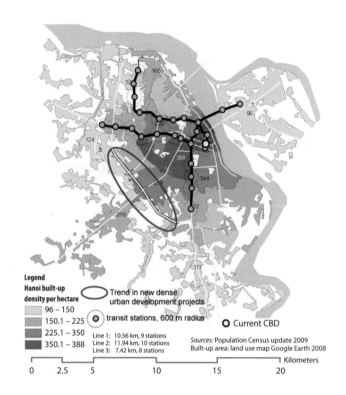

Legend

Hanoi built-up density per hectare

◯ Trend in new dense urban development projects

96 – 150

150.1 – 225   ⊚ transit stations, 600 m radius   ◯ Current CBD

225.1 – 350   Line 1: 10.56 km, 9 stations

350.1 – 388   Line 2: 11.94 km, 10 stations   *Sources:* Population Census update 2009
                 Line 3:   7.42 km, 8 stations   Built-up area: land use map Google Earth 2008

                                                                                        Kilometers
0   2.5   5   10   15   20

Source: World Bank 2011.

the metropolis of Kampala, Uganda urgently needs a credible system for documenting and valuing land. To be sure, local urban bodies also need financing support—to buy land and pay for infrastructure. But no amount of financing alone will solve Uganda's problems.

The Republic of Korea can be considered a model of success, where urban planning and land management institutions have evolved to meet challenges at each stage of urbanization. Land development programs were established first, followed by a land use regulation system. Then came comprehensive urban planning, with guidelines for mandatory 20-year visions, zoning decisions, and planning facilities. Downtown development projects systematically adhered to phased scenarios under the comprehensive plans. Later, in the 1990s and 2000s, Korea integrated separate laws regulating urban and non-urban areas, and in 2000 it instituted metropolitan city–regional planning (between the city and the county or province). Meanwhile, the government initiated large-scale apartment construction projects that solved Korea's most serious urban housing problems. Multiple transport modes were developed. Road projects, over time, have included urban highways and pavement projects as well as a network of expressways. And the nation's rail network includes urban subway lines alongside traditional railroads and high-speed rail—the bullet trains that have shrunk Korea into a half-day travel zone.

Planning, connecting, and financing need to be integrated—as they are in this report, with chapters 1–3 drawing lessons from previous and ongoing Urbanization Reviews. In addition, chapter 4 presents the plan-connect-finance framework in action, distilling lessons from pilots in seven countries (Brazil, China, Colombia, India, Indonesia, Korea, and Vietnam), with lessons from each. Interleaved with the chapters are four spotlights that apply the framework to ongoing policy debates. They discuss slums and natural hazards (spotlight A), infrastructure service provision (spotlight B), new growth poles and urban regeneration (spotlight C), and innovations in municipal finance (spotlight D).

City leaders can use the three-dimensional urban development framework and the case studies in this report to tailor the analysis and identify the impediments to urbanization in their cities and countries—assessing "where the shoe really pinches." Then they can identify the policy options that are most politically, technically, and fiscally feasible. What are the specific tasks under planning, connecting, and financing that policy makers should focus on? Consider three more terms that are also commonly used: value, coordinate, and leverage—terms that can help sharpen the effectiveness of planning, connecting, and financing.

Planning cities

Planning is fundamental to agglomeration economies in three ways. First, land use requires effective systems for land valuation. Second, land use must be allocated in a way that allows for infrastructure improvements. Third, the most basic infrastructure services—water, energy, sanitation, and solid waste management—need to be provided for all residents, urban and peri-urban alike.

Value the city's land by establishing systematic and transparent assessment

Urbanization generates an increase in the demand for land, and a problem arises when land is scarce in places it is needed the most. The success of tools for accommodating urban expansion and redevelopment is typically based on robust systems for assessing land values. And a clear definition of property rights is a first requirement in this direction. Further, developed countries rely on various forms of data and institutions to assess land values, including market data on transactions and attributes of the property, as well as ancillary data on potential income from land and the cost of inputs into land development. These data are managed to provide up-to-date and reliable information for professional appraisers as well as the general public. Institutions that improve the information foundations of the valuation process, including a trained cadre of appraisers in property valuation, contribute to ensuring transparency in the valuation process and to making information on land values widely accessible.

To establish appraised land values and prevent land-related conflict, city leaders should promote valuation processes that are systematic, professional, and transparent. Consider Korea, which during the 1970s encouraged the development of a cadre of property appraisers—bringing transparency to the valuation process while making information on land values widely accessible. In previous land acquisitions, market values and asset replacement costs had been assessed by local government officials. In 1972, the government introduced the Basic Land Prices system, which mandated the assessment of land and buildings by certified private appraisers. Estimated property values from two appraisers were averaged for a final value; if the two appraisals differed by more than 10 percent, a third private appraiser was selected and a new average calculated (World Bank 2013).

Although the valuation of land is essential to the efficient allocation of land use, many developing countries lack institutions for valuing land effectively. In countries where land values are concealed to avoid high transaction taxes, or are distorted by laws that allow developers to acquire land at favorable rates, the result is inefficiency: land may not be allocated to the best use, high prices may lead to affordability problems, and infrastructure expansion may face delays because land is not easily accessible. Take India, where such information systems are in their infancy and the government often acquires land for industrial and infrastructure development. Farmers and other landowners are compensated with payments benchmarked on the stamp duties—a land transaction tax. But since the marginal rate for stamp duties historically has been as high as 12 percent, land and property values have long been underreported. Now, as India's policy makers amend the rules for changes in land use, the lack of independent and reliable land valuations is likely to generate public discontent and related conflicts.

But building these institutions may take time, and second-best solutions may help countries in the interim as longer-term objectives are pursued. In India, for example, while stronger institutions governing land use conversion, property rights definition and adjudication, and land valuation emerge and land markets mature over time, city leaders may want to look at alternative options for the short and medium term. In India, leaders could explore expanding the use of land readjustment[3] methods for land assembly and infrastructure development in urban areas.

Coordinate land management with infrastructure, natural resources, and hazard risk

A city's demand for physical structures, infrastructure, housing, and amenities will change with time as its population grows. To meet new demand, city leaders and planners must have strategies that are flexible. Otherwise their decisions and policies can lock cities into physical forms that may prove suboptimal. For example, density limits—though important—should not impede economic growth or prevent the development of affordable urban housing. Bangalore is an example of density regulations reducing economic efficiency. Research shows that if the city's density restrictions were lifted, its radius would be 8 kilometers rather than the present 12, so the city would grow in a more compact form. Commuting times would shrink, saving households about 4 percent of their income through lower transport costs (Bertaud and Brueckner 2004).

Similarly, land use policies need to be aligned with infrastructure plans (such as plans for public transit). Singapore is a good example: densities vary by location, planned use, and infrastructure availability (with higher densities near metro stations). New York varies densities block by block and by planned use—commercial areas in midtown and downtown Manhattan have much higher densities than do uptown residential areas. To fund infrastructure improvements, cities can sell developers the right to build at higher densities than would otherwise be allowed in a given location. Aligning land use and infrastructure can also help manage the formation and growth of slums (see spotlight A). In Tunisia, the national upgrading program has dramatically reduced slum housing from 23 percent in 1975 to 2 percent in 1995 of the overall housing stock. The program was successful as national utilities made massive investments in water and sewer trunk infrastructure over the same period, making it possible to upgrade existing informal settlements.

In thinking about coordinating land use policies with infrastructure plans, it is also important to consider vulnerability to natural hazard risks. While 70 percent of high-income countries integrate land use and natural risk management, only about 15 percent of low-income countries are doing so (World Bank 2012b). This is of concern as cities are more vulnerable to natural hazards, including floods that are becoming more destructive in many parts of the world. Equally important is coordination between land use and natural resource management—including water resources and water supply (World Bank 2012c). Swakopmund, Namibia, a city of 42,000 surrounded by environmentally sensitive areas, has been able to limit development to within the zoned "townlands" and has protected watersheds through integrated environmental, sector, and land use planning.

Leverage competitive markets alongside regulation to expand basic infrastructure

Water, sanitation, transportation, and electricity are basic services. How can city leaders promote their expansion and increase access? For certain services—such as trucking—it is possible to establish wholly competitive markets, with free entry to providers and prices that reflect demand while covering costs. For other services, such as bus transportation and garbage removal, the effects of competition can be mimicked through recurrent auctions: franchises go to the provider who offers the lowest price for a given set of performance criteria.

Such franchise auctions have succeeded in reducing both costs and prices, so they deserve serious consideration. In many cities, such as Bogotá, London, and Santiago, bus routes are auctioned to operators who are then assigned to predefined itineraries. In London, since auctions were instituted, operating costs per bus-kilometer have declined considerably (gross of administrative costs by an estimated 20–35 percent, net of administrative costs by at least 14 percent) (Estache and Gomez-Lobo 2004). Santiago awards five-year contracts using criteria that include the fare offered by the bidder, along with performance standards. Before the auctions, during a period of deregulation, bus fares had risen; with the auctions, the fares came back down.

For still other services, characterized by natural monopolies (networks) and public good characteristics, such as provision of water and sanitation, governments and city leaders have to set realistic objectives for the development of the water supply and sanitation sector, checked against available resources and agreed on in a multistakeholder policy dialogue. Efforts to improve the effectiveness of service delivery and lower capital costs are needed in most cities. These efforts may be supported by a range of planning tools including strategic financial planning, legislative and regulatory reform, benchmarking, and performance tools.

In addition, prices may have to be regulated. But to make regulatory regimes work, cities need a mechanism to prevent after-the-fact opportunism—by regulators or by service providers. In Latin America, for example, providers have renegotiated 55 percent of infrastructure concessions in transport and 75 percent in water and sanitation.

Finally, price discrimination and subsidies can be used to expand access to services such as public transportation—for both social equity and environmental sustainability. Still, city leaders should look first at market structures that give providers the needed incentives and flexibility to cover costs while serving as many people as possible.

Connecting cities

Connections—between cities and within cities—benefit producers and consumers. They give producers access to input (including labor) and output markets. They give consumers options and, in many cases, better prices. And connections expose cities to new economic opportunities. But city leaders who envision better transport connections for cities and neighborhoods face difficult choices. With limited resources, they cannot invest in everything. It is hard to know which new or improved connections will yield the highest returns over time.

Setting priorities for connective investment means picking winners and losers in the short run—but in the long run, thinking about priorities can make a vast difference for cities, even countries. To identify the most effective additions and improvements to the networks connecting cities and neighborhoods, city leaders can take the following three steps.

Value the city's external and internal connections

For external connections, compare a city's transport costs—and the density, quality, and capacity of roads, railways, waterways, and the like—with data from similar cities. In this way, determine where improvement is most needed. Alternatively, identify possible transport cost reductions and connectivity gains that reflect the city's desired mix of economic activities and extent of specialization. In Colombia, lowering transport costs along the country's key trade corridors can enhance competitiveness—for cities and for the nation. For example, transporting freight by road from Bogotá to the Atlantic costs about $94 per ton while maritime transport from the Colombian coast to the United States is less, at about $75 per ton. High domestic transport costs undermine the competitiveness of goods produced in Colombia's largest cities, especially compared with other large cities around the world. Reducing domestic transport costs by 12 percent can lead to an increase in exports of about 9 percent (Blyde and Martincus 2011).

For internal connections, find out what the problems are: are gridlocks and lack of adequate public transport deterring residents from working outside their immediate neighborhoods (making labor markets inefficient)? Conversely, are long commuting times or high fares forcing residents to live in crowded slums so that they can walk to work? A city that faces one or both of these challenges needs a plan for a better transport system, including a desired mix of transportation modes. The plan must balance two main objectives: increasing the supply of affordable transport options, and ensuring that congestion and pollution remain within acceptable limits.

Coordinate among transport options and with land use

From the beginning, city leaders must systematically coordinate transport plans with land use policies and related infrastructure plans.

Different cities demand different modal mixes, different neighborhoods demand different modes: mass transport is generally suited to compact areas, private vehicles to more sprawling ones.

City leaders should also seek ways to reduce the gap between transport prices and costs—both between cities and within them—by inducing competition in transport markets. Not all modes and routes will support multiple providers. But where they will, and where demand is high enough, policies and regulations should foster competition and not create artificial monopolies. At the same time, city leaders should find ways to price the full cost of individual motor vehicle use. These costs include externalities from congestion where road users do not take account of the time costs they incur on other road users (Kopp 2007). Local air pollution imposes additional costs. The expansion of urban areas separates jobs and residential locations, increasing trip lengths and use of motorized transport. The associated health costs are high—in Beijing, the health costs from local air pollution are estimated at $3.5 billion annually (Creutzig and He 2009).

Finally, city leaders must balance the aim of covering transport costs through market pricing with other social and environmental objectives. In Brazil, the government requires formal sector employers to provide transit tickets to their employees through a system called *vale transporte* (transportation vouchers, VT); the firms then deduct the VT expenditures from taxable income. The VT system—albeit affecting only the formal sector—effectively spreads the cost of transport subsidies between employers and the government.

If city leaders were to convey all the external effects of transport to users, monetary costs of transport would increase. This would gradually make households and firms rebalance their decisions on where to live and where to establish business. The result would be a denser settlement pattern, higher land rents, and shorter transport distances—contributing to the efficiency of cities.

Leverage investments that will yield the highest returns for cities—collectively and individually

Nationally, leaders must identify the most efficient investments in connections among all the cities in a country. Where is demand highest for the expansion of intercity infrastructure and transport services? Which corridors are identified through spatial analysis and simulations as most central to the network, in that improving them will yield the highest returns—for efficiency and for equity? Similarly, leaders must find ways to make transport within cities affordable while limiting congestion and pollution. Investments to increase capacity should be combined and aligned with other policies. Targeted subsidies, though not effective for all purposes or in all contexts, can sometimes be used to make transport more efficient as well as more equitable and safer for the environment. And other fiscal and regulatory tools can be used to manage demand for particular transport modes.

Financing cities

How do city leaders bridge the gap between readily available resources and investment needs? What sources should they tap? To start with, the government can establish its creditworthiness by first securing cash flows from user fees and taxes—and by leveraging the value of land in several ways, including taxes. Only after that can the government begin to borrow money and attract private investment, making finance easier. Whether financing is public or private generally does not make the difference between successful and struggling cities. But there are at least two situations in which private financing may be the preferred course: when the government sees public-private partnerships as a way to improve efficiency in service provision, and when the government suffers from severe credit constraints that prevent it from obtaining credit for improvements to publicly run systems.

Value and develop the city's creditworthiness

Without domestic credit markets, and often lacking the transparency needed in municipal bond markets, many city governments in developing countries cannot access long-term credit. Experience shows that subnational debt can work if clear regulations are in place to:

* Guide the issuance of debt.
* Manage risks from borrowing.
* Clearly set forth the conditions for subnational governments to issue debt (including the purpose, type, and amount of debt that can be issued).[4]

To make the issuance of debt to cities more transparent, Colombia has published traffic-light ratings of local government payment capacity, with red, green, and yellow signals reflecting a combination of liquidity and solvency indicators. To rate municipalities' subnational debt, a red light identifies those whose ratio of interest to operational savings exceeds 40 percent and whose ratio of debt stock to current revenues exceeds 80 percent. Red-light municipalities cannot borrow. Green-light municipalities can. Yellow-light municipalities can borrow only after obtaining the approval of the central government.

Creditworthiness is limited not only to local governments—it extends to their utility companies. In Kenya, the Water Services Regulatory Board calculated and published utility shadow credit ratings for 43 water service providers in 2011 and found only 13 providers to have investment grade ratings.

Smaller cities can seek short- and medium-term loans from higher levels of government and pool their credit. Thus, governments of smaller cities can use bond banks, loan pools, and guarantees to reduce lenders' risks. There are two common types of municipal bonds: general obligation bonds—debt instruments secured by general purpose municipal revenue such as property taxes—and revenue bonds—debt instruments secured by the revenue generated from specific municipal assets (such as ports, toll roads, water and wastewater utilities), with or without recourse to general revenues. Revenue bonds are particularly useful in cases where bond markets are not well developed. Colombia, India, Malaysia, Romania, the Russian Federation, the Slovak Republic, Slovenia, South Africa, and the República Bolivariana de Venezuela provide examples of countries where cities have raised funds from municipal bonds.

In the absence of a well-developed bond market, financial intermediaries in diverse forms play important roles in mobilizing resources for urban infrastructure financing. In Colombia, a successful financial intermediary is FINDETER (Financiera de Desarrollo Territorial), a government company created to finance regional urban infrastructure projects. More than 90 percent owned by the national government, with the remainder owned by the regions (Departments), FINDETER provides resources for financial intermediaries who assign them to regional authorities. It has received funds from multilateral banks and has consistently received high credit ratings (Samad, Lozano-Gracia, and Panman 2012). Still, none of these methods can replace a creditworthy local government.

Coordinate public and private finance using clear and consistent rules

When city governments have constrained access to credit, private investors may step in to fill the gap. There are many types of partnership structures, with each one transferring different levels of risk to the private sector. They include service contracts, management contracts, leases, and privatization. Under any of these structures, property rights must first be clearly defined, so that creditors need not depend on the government's promises. Then a public-private partnership, with private sector selection mechanisms based on the market and on cost-benefit analyses, can improve project selection and ensure project sustainability while adding sources of infrastructure financing. Nevertheless, public-

private partnerships (PPPs) are no magic bullet: they require commitments to sustainable cost-covering tariffs or equivalent tax revenues. They cannot stand in for good financial management or good project evaluation. Clear rules must dictate the procedures, the requirements, the approvals, the institutional responsibilities of the entities involved, and the allocation of risk.

Consider Ghana, where such rules were not in place. In 2002, the government of Ghana initiated a process to encourage PPPs in the urban water sector. However, lack of transparency and accusations of corruption in the selection process led to the end of the PPP. And in Bolivia, the government privatized the water supply system in the city of Cochabamba, awarding a 40-year concession to the private consortium, *Aguas del Tunari*. The contract was awarded without adequate appraisal of the financial situation of the company. Once the concession was awarded, rate structures were modified resulting in an increase of up to $20 in water bills, representing as much as 20 percent of incomes for local families. Subsequent violent protests led to *Aguas del Tunari* withdrawing from the project (Cuttaree 2008; World Bank Institute and PPIAF 2012).

In contrast, Chile put in place a clear and transparent procurement process, focusing on public awareness and a learning-by-doing approach that allowed for adjustments along the way. This process led to the award of 21 road projects on a competitive basis between 1993 and 2001 (Hodge 2006). The bidding started with smaller projects in order to test the market while also minimizing the risk for the private sector. More than 40 Chilean and international companies from 10 countries participated in the bidding through 27 consortia.

To successfully implement PPPs, city leaders will have to consider strengthening public sector capacity, laying out the appropriate legal and sector framework, promoting rigorous planning and risk assessment through feasibility studies, ensuring transparent and competitive procurement, building strong monitoring systems, and allowing flexibility for adapting to unpredictable events.

Leverage existing assets to develop new ones, linking both to land use planning

Land sales and leaseholds can provide initial capital for new infrastructure investments. Sales in Cairo, Istanbul, and Mumbai provide examples of the revenue potential of land auctions. Yet in the long run, governments must tap own source revenues such as property taxes, or similar levies, and access long-term credit to fund the maintenance and expansion of public facilities. Of special interest are three revenue sources—betterment levies, special assessment taxes, and exactions—that link fees to increases in land value based on infrastructure improvements. All these ways to leverage state assets require the presence of many factors to succeed, and all have risks. Strong institutions are essential to make these instruments work. Institutions to clearly define property rights, to objectively value land using standard methods, and to support and oversee land management, land sales, and tax collection.

Planning, connecting, and financing cities—now

Urbanization in today's developed countries occurred gradually, over a hundred years or more. That fairly leisurely pace allowed for trial and error in the development of rules and capabilities. In contrast, today's developing countries face sudden deluges from the countryside. Some can expect to go from 10–20 percent urban population to 60–85 percent in just 30 years.

Such rapid urbanization confronts developing country governments with unprecedented institutional and fiscal challenges. Managing individual decisions and planning for urbanization, today's cities struggle to ensure the availability of shelter, transport, and other basic infrastructure and services. All are needed by growing populations—and they are needed by businesses to start and expand.

BOX O.2   Planning, connecting, and financing cities: How the World Bank can help city leaders

The World Bank has instruments to help city leaders plan, connect, and finance for the future.

Planning. To support evidence-based urban planning policy at the national and city levels, the World Bank can build on:

- City Asset Management Strategies (with robust data collection and dissemination).
- Municipal Contracts (with tools to capture multicity data, as part of a wholesaling approach).
- Subnational Investment Climate Assessments and Doing Business Surveys (with greater coverage).

The Bank can also use the Urbanization Knowledge Platform and its Singapore and Marseille Urban Hubs to support city leaders with just-in-time advice.

Connecting. To support improved connections through Development Policy Loans at the subnational level—with its focus on housing and slums, land and urban poverty, and urban mobility—the Bank can expand programmatic and policy-based lending. It is also exploring options for results-based programmatic lending linked to core elements of planning and connecting cities.

Financing. To partly cover debt servicing for governments borrowing from commercial markets (loans and bonds) and so improve debt terms, the Bank can provide policy-based guarantees—resulting in longer maturities, lower interest rates, higher debt limits, and the power to tap new markets and institutional investors.

For the economy, for equity, and for sustainability, it is therefore of the greatest urgency that city leaders plan, connect, and finance their cities—now. How decision makers prepare for rapid urbanization is crucial, not only to the future of their cities, but also to global economic progress and sustainability. The World Bank, among others, can help (box O.2).

Notes

1. These are concerns expressed by more than 750 city leaders in regional and national consultations on urbanization priorities carried out through the Urbanization Knowledge Platform—a global partnership for open-source knowledge exchange among policy makers, practitioners, and researchers. The platform included countries ranging from low to high income, from the smallest country size to the largest.
2. See Clark (forthcoming) for a discussion on who constitutes city leaders and what *leadership* implies.
3. Land readjustment is, in essence, a participatory tool used for land assembly and infrastructure development. In India, it has been applied under the name of Town Planning Schemes in the State of Gujarat.
4. This includes national government clearing of subnational borrowing.

References

Bertaud, Alain. 2009. "Note on Spatial Issues in Urban South Africa." http://alain-bertaud .com/AB_Files/_vti_cnf/AB_Note%20on%20 South%20Africa.pdf.

Bertaud, Alain, and Jan K. Brueckner. 2004. "Analyzing Building-Height Restrictions: Predicted Impacts Welfare Costs, and a Case Study of Bangalore, India." Policy Research Working Paper 3290, World Bank, Washington, DC.

Blyde, J., and C. Volpe Martincus. 2011. "Shaky Roads and Trembling Exports: Assessing the Trade Effects of Domestic Transport Costs Using a Natural Experiment." Paper presented at the Forum for Research in Empirical International Trade, Ljubljana, Slovak Republic, June 9–11. http://www.freit.org/LETC/2011/ SubmittedPapers/Christian_Volpe_Martincus74.pdf.

Clark, Greg. Forthcoming. "Leadership and Governance." In *Rethinking Cities*, ed. Edward Glaeser and Abha Joshi Ghani. Washington, DC: World Bank.

Creutzig, Felix, and Dongquan He. 2009. "Climate Change Mitigation Policies and Co-benefits of Feasible Transport Demand Policies in Beijing." *Transportation Research Part D* 14 (2): 120–31.

Cuttaree, Vickram. 2008. "Successes and Failures of PPP Projects." World Bank, Europe and Central Asia Region, Warsaw. http:// site resources.worldbank.org/INTECARE GTOPTRANSPORT/Resources/Day1_Pres2_ SuccessesandFailuresPPPprojects15JUN08.ppt.

Estache, Antonio, and Andres Gomez-Lobo. 2004. "The Limits to Competition in Urban Bus Services in Developing Countries." Policy Research Working Paper 3207, World Bank, Washington, DC.

Hallegatte, Stéphane. 2009. "Strategies to Adapt to an Uncertain Climate Change." *Global Environmental Change* 19 (2): 240–7.

Hodge, Graeme A. 2006. "Public-Private Partnerships and Legitimacy." *University of New South Wales Law Journal* 29 (3): 318–27.

Kopp, Andreas. 2007. "Summary and Discussion." In *Transport Infrastructure Charges and Capacity Choice. Self-financing Road Maintenance and Construction*. ECMT Round Table Report 135. Paris: Organisation for Economic Co-operation and Development.

Samad, Taimur, Nancy Lozano-Gracia, and Alexandra Panman. 2012. *Colombia Urbanization Review: Amplifying the Gains from Urban Transition*. Directions in Development Series. Washington, DC: World Bank.

World Bank. 2008. *World Development Report: Reshaping Economic Geography*. Washington, DC: World Bank.

———. 2009a. *World Development Indicators (CD-ROM)*. Washington, DC: World Bank.

———. 2010. "System of Cities: Harnessing Urbanization for Growth and Poverty Reduction." Finance, Economics, and Urban Department, Urban and Local Governments Unit, Washington, DC.

———. 2011. "Vietnam Urbanization Review." Technical Assistance Report. The World Bank. Washington, DC.

———. 2012a. *Eurasian Cities: New Realities along the Silk Road*. Washington, DC: World Bank.

———. 2012b. *Inclusive Green Growth: The Pathway to Sustainable Development*. Washington, DC: World Bank.

———. 2012c. *The Future of Water in African Cities: Why Waste Water?* Washington, DC: World Bank.

———. 2013. *Urbanization beyond Municipal Boundaries: Nurturing Metropolitan Economies and Connecting Peri-urban Areas in India*. Directions in Development Series. Washington, DC: World Bank.

World Bank Institute and PPIAF (Public-Private Infrastructure Advisory Facility). 2012. *Public-Private Partnerships Reference Guide. Version 1.0*. Washington, DC: World Bank.

Planning cities

Cities thrive when people and firms can benefit from being close together, creating agglomeration economies. But this beneficial transformation can be thwarted by policies that stymie development in urban areas. One obstacle arising from bad policy is inefficiency in the use and exchange of land. Another is a lack of coordination between land use and infrastructure planning. To overcome these obstacles requires three sets of policies:

- *Value the city's land by establishing systematic and transparent assessment.* Because land use shapes a city's spatial structure, cities need policies that clearly define property rights and determine land values. With such policies in place, urban land markets help to mediate between demand and supply, increasing land utilization and optimizing the development of constructed floor area.
- *Coordinate land management with infrastructure, natural resources, and hazard risk.* Cities need policies to govern the intensity of land use and to manage its integration with infrastructure development—especially transport.
- *Leverage competitive markets alongside regulation to expand basic infrastructure.*

Cities need policies for the provision of public goods and basic infrastructure services (water, sanitation, and solid waste management). In developing countries, access to these services tends to be especially low in smaller cities and on the fringes of metropolitan cities.

Value the city's land by establishing systematic and transparent assessment

The use and reuse of land is central to a city's expansion and development. For economic efficiency, land should be able to shift among various uses—though public intervention may be required to offset market failures (Henderson and Wang 2007). Urban land markets should efficiently allocate land between urban and rural uses (with incentives to conserve farmland and green space) and within urban areas (to prevent disordered land use and underserved neighborhoods).

What is the key to efficient land use? The answer is the price of land. Developed countries determine the price and value of land by examining property attributes and market data from transactions. Developing countries cannot do this so long as they lack certain basic institutions, as well as ancillary data concerning potential income from land, and the cost of inputs into land development. These data are managed to provide up-to-date and reliable information for professional appraisers as well as the general public. Consider the Republic of Korea, which during the 1970s encouraged the development of a cadre of property appraisers—bringing transparency to the valuation process while making information on land values widely accessible. In previous land acquisitions, market values and asset replacement costs had been assessed by local government officials. In 1972, the government introduced the Basic Land Prices system, which mandated the assessment of land and buildings by certified private appraisers. Estimated property values from two appraisers were averaged for a final value; if the two appraisals differed by more than 10 percent, a third private appraiser was selected and a new average calculated (World Bank 2013).

Many developing countries often lack the systems to record and manage this information. Transaction data, for instance, may not reflect the true price of land because of informal market transactions to save on duties or heavy public subsidies on housing and land use. Land registries are often archaic and lack the dynamic functionality that allows them to be searched or updated quickly. These deficient features in transaction record management translate to a dearth of data on real estate prices, preventing analysis that is critical for land value appraisal. The implications of this bear heavily on local financing mechanisms involving real estate and infrastructure.

Land valuation is integral to local revenue generation since land values form the basis for activities such as property tax collection and land sales or leases. A credible system that helps "discover" and "disseminate" the value of land makes it difficult for buyers to defraud existing landowners. In the absence of such information, there is considerable scope for undervaluation of land during the acquisition process.

Take India, where such information systems are in their infancy and the government often acquires land for industrial and infrastructure development. Farmers and other landowners are compensated with payments benchmarked on the stamp duties—a land transaction tax. But since the marginal rate for stamp duties historically has been as high as 12 percent, land and property values have long been underreported (World Bank 2013).[1] Now, as India's policy makers amend the rules for changes in land use, the lack of independent and reliable land valuations is likely to result in public discontent and conflicts over land.

In Vietnam, too, official land prices fail to reflect demand. The country has two kinds of prices for land transactions. First, there is the market price—the higher of the two. Then there is the imposed land price—a much lower value, used by the government in acquiring land and allocating it to developers and investors (World Bank 2011f). Such an inequitable system generates resentment over land acquisitions: over 1996–2005, there were more than 12,000 complaints. And conflicts over land, in turn, hinder the consolidation of plots for industrial development. More than 85 percent of available plots in Vietnam are smaller than 20 hectares—but industrial parks and districts typically need 150–200 hectares of contiguous land (figure 1.1). So the country's two-price system impedes efficiency and economic development.

In countries that have created successful industrial parks, these areas are much larger. An example is Shenzhen, China—the most thriving special economic zone in the country, and among the world's most successful examples of an integrated growth center and magnet for foreign investment. In 2005, Shenzhen comprised more than 70,000 hectares (Lei and Bin 2008). And in Indonesia, which has deconcentrated industrial activities out of the cores of Jakarta and Surabaya, industrial districts range from 500–800 hectares (World Bank 2011b).

City leaders in Bogotá recently pioneered the improvement of land valuation. Between 2008 and 2010, the city updated its cadastral database, revaluing the 2.1 million properties it contains—generating a new revenue stream

FIGURE 1.1   Vietnam's dual land price system creates problems for the assembly of large plots of land needed for industry

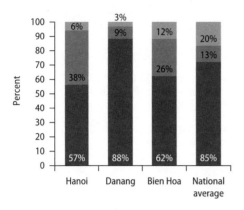

Source: World Bank 2011f.

FIGURE 1.2   Bottlenecks in accessing industrial land for private investment

Source: Data from Doing Business 2012 Survey.

of $171 million annually (Ruiz and Vallejo 2010). To complete the cadastral update, the government introduced information technology, consulted with stakeholders, and began estimating property values using spatially detailed information from geographic information systems (GIS) (Uribe 2010). Since no property transaction information was available, a team of expert appraisers collected price data using a combination of approaches to yield an appraised value. But to keep property taxes progressive—and to avoid resistance from property owners—the city imposed a cap on property tax increases. Similarly, it is generally recognized in the United States that tax assessors' calculation of property value is about 33 percent lower than market value.

Obstacles to valuing and assembling land make it hard for firms to explore agglomeration economies and hard for governments to provide rights-of-way and basic services. About two in five firms in Algeria, Lebanon, and Morocco identify the difficulty of access

to suitable land (zoned and serviced for industry) as a major business constraint. And in India, about one in two firms reports that its greatest business development challenge is to obtain land in its desired industrial zone.[2] In South Asia, it takes 100 days to lease public land for industrial purposes—the longest wait worldwide (figure 1.2). (In high-income Organisation for Economic Co-operation and Development countries it takes just 26 days.)

In accommodating industry, infrastructure, and urban development, city leaders should first think about improving their institutions for land information and valuation. They can do so by:

- Training a cadre of appraisers in property valuation.
- Ensuring transparency in the valuation process.
- Making information on land values widely accessible.

So long as institutions cannot consistently and accurately discover and disseminate land values, signals to developers and entrepreneurs will be weak—and tensions with landowners will rise. To enable the government—as well as other interested private parties—to value land correctly is to lay the bedrock for complementary policies and investments.

Coordinate land management with infrastructure, natural resources, and hazard risk to reflect market needs and societal preferences

Linked to the functioning of a city's land markets is its demand for physical structures, infrastructure, housing, and amenities. That demand will change over time, requiring city leaders and planners to adapt.

Once the physical structures of a city have been built, though, they are generally fixed for a long time. Urban structures typically survive for more than 100 years—buildings and housing from 20 to 150 years, transport infrastructure from 30 to 200 years (Hallegatte 2009). Such structures will determine how the city's land can be used and reused, dictating whether the urban economy can take full advantage of agglomeration and can contribute to social equity and environment sustainability (box 1.1).

City leaders, therefore, must make careful decisions about their cities' physical structures today—to avoid locking them into physical forms that will be regretted tomorrow. City leaders often are vexed with two different but interrelated problems. First, they need to accommodate new demographic and economic growth, and this may best be located on "greenfield" areas that are not urbanized. And second, they need to revitalize and reorient their cities to modernize them, making them more attractive to businesses and residents. Additionally, a global survey of cities indicates that population densities are falling and that, as the developing country cities continue to grow, they will require much more land. Therefore, many cities are exploring how to manage their densities so that they can minimize urban sprawl.

Managing densities

Land use planning does much to determine urban density, which in turn drives much of the demand for urban infrastructure and largely determines a city's functional efficiency (Levy 2011). Density regulations—one of the tools used most frequently by urban planners—cap the quantity of property that can be developed on a plot of land. Such a cap is often called the floor space index (FSI) or floor area ratio (FAR). So, for example, if the FSI in an area of a city is 1:1, it means that developers can only build a building whose total floor space on the parcel is less than or equal to the total plot area. While in some cases it may be possible to build a one-story building on a plot that entirely covers the plot, and therefore achieves an FSI of 1:1, developers will typically build a building with a "footprint" or "plinth" that covers less than 100 percent of the site, but they will build more than a one-story structure. For example, a developer could cover 25 percent of a plot and build a four-story building and still meet the FSI regulation of 1:1.

Other planning regulations include setbacks (minimum distances to the front, rear, and sides of a plot) and maximum building heights. Both are designed to protect adjacent properties and preserve access to sun, air, and open space (parks and plazas). Finally, plot coverage ratio regulations limit the total area of a plot that can be developed (Dowall 2012; World Bank 2013). It is very important to highlight that there is no such thing as an optimal FSI. The "right" FSI for a specific area will depend on the existing spatial structure of the city, the street patterns and widths, the level of infrastructure (is there enough capacity to accommodate higher density—higher FSIs?), and cultural and social factors (are skyscrapers acceptable?) (Bertaud 2004).

Although these regulations exist for good reasons, they often have unintended consequences. If an area's FSI is set far below the level at which investors might otherwise develop it (assuming an unregulated market), this repression of supply can push people out

BOX 1.1   Greening city growth: Coordinating land use and infrastructure planning

Urban development decisions are long-lived. As such, they create substantial inertia in socioeconomic systems. Because the economic system reorganizes itself around infrastructure and urban plans, and because so much of current growth is in cities, this inertia can extend over centuries. A delay in greening city investments may therefore prove costly if it results in a lock-in into technologies that turn out to no longer be appropriate (because of their excessive carbon, land, or water intensity) or settlement patterns that prove vulnerable to changing climatic conditions.

Developing countries, which still face a huge transport infrastructure gap, have the opportunity to choose their urban forms and their transport development path: low-emission transport or car-dependent transport. Experience suggests that demand for car ownership increases dramatically at annual household incomes of $6,000–$8,000. If history repeats itself, an additional 2.3 billion cars will be added by 2050, mostly in developing countries, given expected economic growth and past patterns of motorization (Chamon, Mauro, and Okawa 2008). Without policies to encourage high-density urbanization and public transport, high reliance on individual car transport will ensue. Consequences would include high congestion—costly in energy expenditure and time lost—and local pollution with significant health impacts.

But if public transport is included as a major part of modal structure in urban transport, there is no conflict between a low-emission transport sector and rapid growth or high income. In fact, economies with some of the lowest ratios of energy consumption to GDP in the world—including Hong Kong SAR, China; Japan; and Singapore—have experienced extraordinary development over the past few decades. Curitiba and Copenhagen are two examples of where the reliance on cars is lower than average:

- The city of Curitiba shows that coordinating urban transport with planning—to concentrate population around public transportation lines and hubs—makes it possible to maximize the share of

trips done with low-energy-consumption modes (Suzuki, Cervero, and Iuchi 2013).
- The city of Copenhagen was designed following a transit-oriented and bike-friendly approach: starting from a "finger plan"—the identification of few priority development areas—then investing in five-axis transit radials and corridors of satellite, rail-served new towns (Cervero 1998).

But in most world cities, the decrease in the relative price of transport by individual car—due to income growth and improved car energy efficiency—has led to decreasing density, increasing sprawl, and rising dependency on individual vehicles.

The consequence of the inertia in urban development is an enormous potential for regret if decisions are made without adequate consideration of how conditions—socioeconomic, environmental, and technological—will change over time. The potential for regret has always been a challenge for policies with long-term implications, but it has been heightened by climate change and the volatility in energy prices. Avoiding these lock-ins—and the corresponding regret or retrofitting costs—should be a priority for making decisions on urban planning and urban infrastructure.

Of course, building better (cleaner, more resilient, or both) can be more expensive. This tradeoff raises the fear that countries faced with severe financing constraints may need to choose between "building right" (which may make both economic and environmental sense) and "building more" (which may be what is required socially). But the additional cost of building greener cities should not be overstated: in the urban sector, the additional cost to build with higher density and with lower energy building—thanks to better insulation and more efficient heating systems—is limited and provides multiple cobenefits, making this domain a priority for immediate action (Viguie and Hallegatte 2012).

Contributed by Stéphane Hallegatte.

to other areas—and the increased demand for those other areas can raise prices across the city (Annez and Linn 2010). Similarly, if the FSI is a uniform limit, it may increase

housing prices by limiting the supply of land that would otherwise be built up. It may also encourage the allocation of land and buildings to less productive uses. Beyond slowing city growth in these ways, a uniform limit can also push poor households to distant suburbs, adding to their poverty by increasing their commuting costs and times. When households have no choice but to locate themselves near jobs, they often join hazard-prone informal settlements (see spotlight A).

Bangalore is an example of density regulations reducing economic efficiency. Its FAR is between 1.75 and 3.25, well below the typical range (most large cities around the world have a FAR between 5 and 15). The result? Research shows that if the city's density restrictions were lifted, its radius would be 8 kilometers rather than the present 12. Commuting times would shrink, saving households about 4 percent of their income through lower transport costs (Bertaud and Brueckner 2004).

By contrast, developers in Bangkok's less restricted land markets were able to adapt to growing demographic and economic pressures and climbing costs. Over 1974–88, when growth was rapid and land and housing construction prices were on the rise, developers responded by increasing the density of their housing projects. The average number of units per hectare rose from 35 to 56, and multifamily housing increased from less than 2 percent of new construction in 1986 to 43 percent in 1990. Such shifts allowed the developers to build affordable housing profitably (Dowall 1992). Over 1986–90, almost half the growth in Bangkok housing stock was from private development, while informally produced housing composed a mere 3 percent of the total. In other cities with highly constrained land markets, informally produced housing composed 20–80 percent of the total (Dowall 1998).

To effectively shape the space, density, and land use pattern of a city or metropolitan area, planners can work with a master plan and structure plan to prepare detailed district plans. They can draft zoning ordinances to aid the plans' implementation. And they can prepare FSI or FAR regulations to limit building density (Dowall 2012). Such density regulations can simultaneously be coordinated with infrastructure plans.

In addition to density regulations, enforcement of land use plans becomes a challenge when local governments do not have the administrative capacity to monitor and facilitate growth of new settlements. In Dakar, the fastest population growth in the metropolitan region over the past 20 years took place in peri-urban areas as they provide cheap and readily available land for settlement. However, 40 percent of the population growth in these areas occurred on land in precarious areas—with the risk exacerbated by lack of planning standards and of adequate infrastructure (Pelling 2003). The physical vulnerability and risk in these peri-urban areas is compounded by their weak institutional capacity.

Coordinating land use and infrastructure planning

A central problem of urban planning is that of matching land use and infrastructure for the best possible outcome. Higher densities generate greater need for infrastructure services (electricity, water, and waste water). But they also support environmental sustainability in being better suited to public transport. To be sure, density must not overwhelm infrastructure. Yet it is equally important not to underuse infrastructure, imposing low density caps where infrastructure can support higher ones.

To see what is at stake, compare Manhattan—New York City's archetypal borough—with Mumbai (map 1.1). Manhattan's density zones are typically small. Its restrictions on land use vary with street width and capacity, with infrastructure capacity, and with historical land use patterns (commercial office districts typically have higher FSIs than residential districts). This granularity helps to make Manhattan a good example of integration between land use and infrastructure.

In contrast, Mumbai's density zones are large—uniform across much of the city—and generally low. India's urban planners justify such low formal densities as necessary to avoid overburdening existing infrastructure, which is severely limited. Rather than

MAP 1.1   New York's planning is granular (and integrated with infrastructure)—Mumbai's is coarse

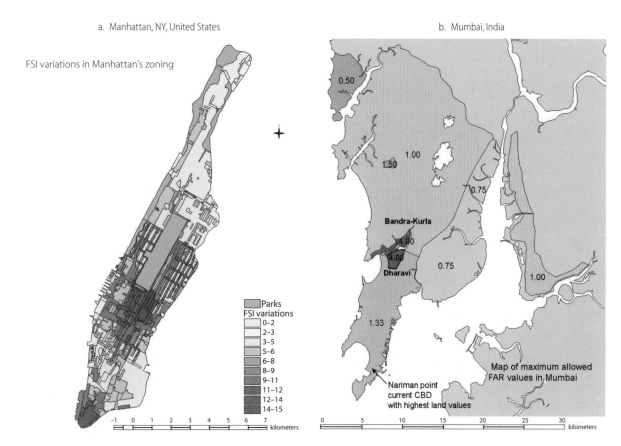

a. Manhattan, NY, United States

FSI variations in Manhattan's zoning

Parks
FSI variations
0–2
2–3
3–5
5–6
6–8
8–9
9–11
11–12
12–14
14–15

b. Mumbai, India

0.50

1.00
1.50

0.75

Bandra-Kurla

4.00
4.00
Dharavi

0.75

1.00

1.33

Nariman point
current CBD
with highest land values

Map of maximum allowed
FAR values in Mumbai

Sources: New York City Planning Department 2011 (left); Bertaud 2004 (right).
Note: In some zones, the floor space index (FSI) might be increased up to two additional units because of bonuses due to plaza, arcades, and the like. In some areas, the permitted FSI might not be reached because of setbacks and plot geometry.

increase formal or planned densities, they have tried to preserve urban areas by pushing development out to new towns and suburban industrial estates (World Bank 2013). But this strategy ignores an opportunity: India's cities could instead use rising land values to finance better, higher-capacity infrastructure, to increase office space and to add affordable housing for low- and moderate-income groups.

Central business districts, and other economically dynamic areas of cities, normally have the highest FSIs. Being well connected to public transit, they can accommodate large daytime populations. But outlying areas adjacent to transit stations—or at major highway intersections—are also given high FSIs by

planners who seek to increase transit use and discourage private motor vehicles. Because a city's transport choices can generate both positive and negative externalities as the city grows, transport is best addressed as part of an integrated urban strategy that can cater to various user groups and anticipate long-term needs. In too many cities, such a strategy has been lacking (World Bank 2002; World Bank 2012a).

Consider Hanoi, where mass transport investments failed to anticipate rising densities. The city expects to complete the first phase of its urban mass rapid transit plan by 2020, meaning that the network and 25 stations will be built (map 1.2, with stations marked in green). In 2009, more than one of

MAP 1.2   Inconsistencies between new development and mass transit investments in Hanoi, Vietnam, 2009

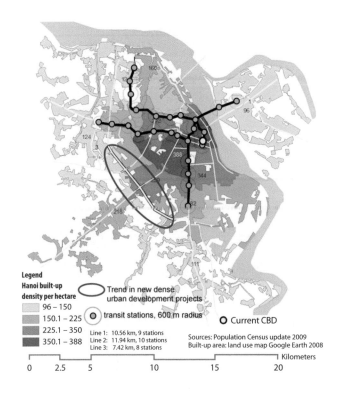

Legend

Hanoi built-up density per hectare

96 – 150	
150.1 – 225	
225.1 – 350	
350.1 – 388	

○ transit stations, 600 m radius

Trend in new dense urban development projects

○ Current CBD

Line 1:   10.56 km, 9 stations
Line 2:   11.94 km, 10 stations
Line 3:   7.42 km, 8 stations

Sources: Population Census update 2009
Built-up area: land use map Google Earth 2008

Kilometers
0   2.5   5   10   15   20

Source: Bertaud 2011,

FIGURE 1.3   São Paulo finances infrastructure improvements by selling land development right

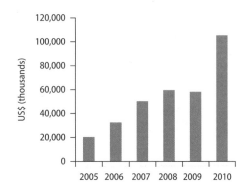

Source: Sandroni 2011.
Note: Annual revenues are from two urban operations (development concessions for additional building rights) in São Paulo.

five residents lived within walking distance of a planned transit station. Yet new developments are now increasing the density of the population along the Pham Hung road in southwest Hanoi—an area that the first phase of the transit network will not serve. As a result, in 2020 a large share of Hanoi's population will be disconnected from the rest of the city.

Cities can use their control over densities to pay for infrastructure, as São Paulo did when it set new rules that integrated land management with infrastructure provision. To balance efficiency with equity, when the city redefined allowable development densities, it imposed a charge for additional building rights even as it capped each area's land supply (World Bank 2011c). The charge for the right to build in a given area was a function of its land and property prices, subjecting land use to economic principles of efficiency.

In two São Paulo localities, Faria Lima and Agua Espraiada, revenues from the sale of additional building rights have been increasing (figure 1.3). The revenues are deposited in a common Urban Development Fund (FUNDURB) that carries out projects defined in the master plan of 2002. So far, most of the revenues have been allocated in two ways: to drainage and sanitation works, and to housing and support for land tenure regularization. A large share of funded improvements is located in the city fringe, implying a redistribution of funds throughout São Paulo: revenues collected in the most dynamic areas are invested in the most deprived, peripheral areas.

Leverage competitive markets alongside regulation to expand basic infrastructure

City leaders need systems for valuing land, and they need land use plans that are coordinated with infrastructure plans. But they also need ways to promote the expansion of urban infrastructure services. The urgency of this need appears in figure 1.4, showing access to piped water for urban residents in

FIGURE 1.4   **Share of population with access to piped water across countries and city sizes**

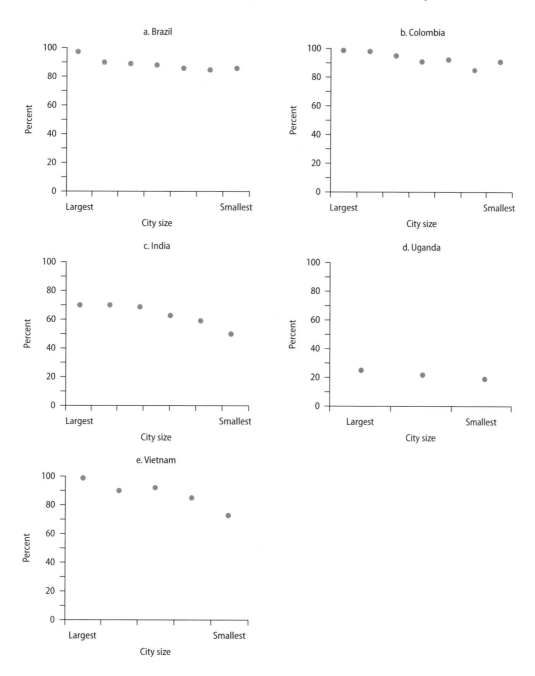

Sources: Brazil: IBGE 2000; Colombia: DANE 2005; India: Ministry of Home Affairs 2001; Uganda: Uganda Bureau of Statistics 2010; Vietnam: General Statistics Office of Vietnam 2009.

Brazil, Colombia, India, Uganda, and Vietnam. In each of these five pilot countries for the World Bank's Urbanization Reviews (see box O.1 in the overview), water access varies with city size—but it does so differently. In Vietnam, access is high but less equitable, with smaller cities showing lower access. In Brazil and Colombia, service coverage is high and fairly equitable. In India and Uganda, access is lower and less equitable.

How to increase access to basic infrastructure services? In most infrastructure services, such as transport, electricity, and telecommunications, a useful question for city leaders is whether there is a framework of clear and consistent rules for service delivery. Three approaches merit consideration:

- *Harness market forces,* either by allowing free competition among providers or by auctioning service franchises (mimicking the effects of competitive pricing through recurrent auctions).
- *Regulate prices,* with mechanisms to insulate the regulators from political influence by the regulated firms.
- *Establish subsidies,* primarily to expand access, when there is no way for prices to cover the costs of equitable service provision.

For services such as water supply and sanitation, the first order considerations are for national governments and city leaders to set realistic objectives for the development of the water supply and sanitation sector, checked against available resources and agreed on in a multistakeholder policy dialogue; to address the governance issues particularly regarding to accountability and public participation; and to address the coordination challenges across sectors and space.

Harnessing market forces

In basic infrastructure, as in other markets, prices ideally should cover costs. Why? Because cost-covering prices are likely to be a city's strongest protection against wasteful investments and consumption.

When policy makers inform potential providers that they will not receive any fiscal transfers or subsidies—but that regulation will allow pricing to cover costs in the aggregate—then providers estimate demand and calibrate it against costs, just as investors in any market would do. Whether the providers are publicly or privately owned makes

no difference: they understand that they will make money only if customers are able and willing to pay the required price.

Can market forces indeed be harnessed—to make basic infrastructure service provision more efficient, to expand access to services, or both (Klein 2012)? Head-to-head competition is feasible in principle for certain sectors: electricity, natural gas, transport, water, and waste management, though the sectors with large expensive networks (electricity, natural gas, rail transport, and water) require elaborate regulation to let service providers share networks.[3] Even where only monopolies are feasible, periodic franchise auctioning can mimic the effects of competitive pricing. However, when large expensive network infrastructure is required, auctioning may be less efficient.

Opportunities to allow free competition

Telecommunications is the most prominent example of a competitive infrastructure market. Others are possible, however.

- In electricity, some competition may be feasible among generators, as well as among energy traders and sellers in larger systems. Hong Kong SAR, China, even left residential prices unregulated until a few years ago. In natural gas, there can be effective competition from competing fuels such as fuel oil. Some systems, such as Germany's, have left prices unregulated and allowed entry into the pipeline business. However, typically duplication of pipelines or creation of a number of adjacent networks with different owners is not economically optimal.
- In transport, various forms of head-to-head competition are possible. Bus and truck companies can compete freely. Ports, or airports, can compete if they are not separated too widely. And freight rail firms may face effective competition from road transport over large distances. In water supply, there may be head-to-head competition. But in most cases, competition between household connections and stand-posts, and alternatives such as

unprotected springs or private wells, may in fact suggest affordability issues or coping strategies to overcome poor infrastructure services.

In some urban services, free market entry is undesirable, because the resulting competition can undermine safety standards. The "penny wars" of Bogotá are an interesting example. Before a bus rapid transit system called TransMilenio was introduced in 2000, about 30,000–35,000 buses were operating in the city (Hook 2005). The government granted nonexclusive permits to the route operators, with whom bus owners were affiliated. The bus owners in turn charged their drivers fixed rents. The drivers' revenue thus depended directly on how many fares they collected (World Bank 2008). Cutthroat competition ensued, with unsafe results: drivers had a strong incentive to speed, cut people off, and carry too many passengers. The introduction of TransMilenio, together with a new regulatory framework, eliminated these "penny wars." The new framework included bidding for all parts of the service, from routes to infrastructure. TransMilenio allocates the market to operators according to their quality, among other factors—and it pays them by the kilometer, assuring them of a certain amount regardless of their passenger load.

Head-to-head competition may also be technically unfeasible in sectors that naturally favor monopolies. Much of a city's networked infrastructure falls in this category: its duplication tends to be inefficient. A single network, fully built out, can often underbid any competitor.[4]

Canada's cities are one example of a natural monopoly superseding market competition. Water utilities would at first compete to supply firms and households in a given market by laying separate pipelines. Then all the providers but one would fade away. In other cases, a monopoly provider started and was not challenged, either because competitors could not undercut it or because entry was forbidden by law. Natural monopolies can also appear in exclusive locations, such as airports and central metro stations.

Yet monopolies can abuse their market power, charging prices that are too high to be socially acceptable. Such prices can also make economies less productive and less competitive. So how can policy allow prices to cover costs—while ensuring that prices stay close to costs, as opposed to fattening a monopoly with excessive profits?

Auctioning service franchises

Regulation can closely mimic the effects of competitive pricing even where monopolies exist. City leaders can auction the right to provide a service for a certain period—moving away from a monopolistic price, and closer to that which would arise from competition. Firms that lose at auction exit the particular market. If it is possible to put such a monopoly franchise up for auction fairly frequently based on the lowest price, the auctions will act like a market to set prices.

Many cities auction bus routes, assigning operators to predefined itineraries. Examples include Santiago, Bogotá, and London. Santiago awards five-year contracts using criteria that include the fare offered by the bidder, along with quality variables. Before the auctions, during a period of deregulation, bus fares had risen; with the auctions, the fares came back down. In London, since auctions were instituted, operating costs per bus-kilometer have declined considerably (gross administrative costs by an estimated 20–35 percent, net administrative costs by at least 14 percent) (Estache and Gomez-Lobo 2004).

Where possible, franchise auctions repeated at intervals of one to three years can make price regulation essentially unnecessary. Such auctions have been used, not only in bus transport, but also in waste management. If a company loses a franchise, its assets—buses, garbage trucks—can be deployed elsewhere.

Regulating prices

Where free entry and auctions are both impractical because of a natural monopoly involving fixed assets in a service area, price regulation is needed.[5] For example, it would be absurd for water providers to remove and replace pipelines after every auction. Nor can such fixed assets be included in the auctions. For an auction to determine the price of a service, the bidder needs to know the price of the assets. And since assets in the ground have negligible market value outside the franchise area, their value depends on the price that the provider can charge—which is what the auction was supposed to determine. Fixing the asset price before the auction would be tantamount to direct regulation of prices.

In regulating prices for basic infrastructure services, the government typically announces a regulatory regime for private or state-owned providers.[6] Only after firms invest does the actual demand become clear. The firms then operate the system to meet demand. Finally, the regulator rules on the revenue that firms can make.

The problem: private providers know that in the last stage of this process—revenue capping—the regulator can renege on the pricing rules announced at first. Such reversals are likely when regulators are under pressure to lower consumer prices or to reduce profits deemed too large. Even in countries with strong legal systems and long regulatory traditions, regulators can be strongly pressured to renege on initially announced pricing rules. In a few parts of the United States where utility regulators are publicly elected, demands to curb prices tend to undermine service provision.

Another problem follows: providers try to renegotiate contracts shortly after the contracts are awarded. In Latin America, providers have renegotiated 55 percent of infrastructure concessions in transport and 75 percent in water and sanitation. The high incidence suggests that this is opportunism—not merely an attempt to compensate for incomplete information in concession contracts. What should be decided through a competitive auction is opportunistically dictated through a bilateral negotiation in which the government, however, lacks power. The benefits of competition thus vanish (Guasch 2004).

In short, wherever the regulatory process is rife with political risk, both private

and state-owned firms will underinvest in basic infrastructure provision. Moreover, firms that win infrastructure contracts will be tempted to renegotiate them. So to make regulatory regimes work, cities need a mechanism to prevent after-the-fact opportunism—either by regulators or by the service providers. Such a mechanism has three parts:

* The design of the pricing rules.
* The legal framework under which rules are made and administered.
* The organizational arrangements for administering the rules.

The design of pricing rules

For prices to cover costs while giving firms an incentive to expand coverage and provide high-quality service, the costs must be calculated—and the prices must allow a rate of return. The danger of after-the-fact expropriation is highest when the regulator imposes a price cap, such as those used in the United Kingdom. Although price caps were meant to give firms an incentive to perform efficiently—allowing them to profit by serving customers well at a lower cost than expected—their profits, once made, were attacked as "too high." Furthermore, caps decouple infrastructure prices from utilization. Even when demand is low, the regulated price will reflect the cost of both used and unused capacity. At such times, regulators may feel pressure to reduce revenues.

Providers have a smaller incentive for efficiency—but may be more willing to invest—when the rate of return is regulated, as in the United States. Profits, rather than prices, are capped after the fact. Regulators can vary this cap, allowing less profit when demand is low and more when demand is high, to make revenues more closely reflect utilization (an instance of the "used and useful" doctrine[7]). An advantage of these typical U.S. arrangements is that they reduce the regulator's incentive to renege. This greater reliability makes investors more likely to put their capital into infrastructure expansion projects, even though prices may fail to cover costs during times of low demand.[8]

In cities in developing countries, basic infrastructure service prices regularly fail to cover the providers' costs. In some of India's largest cities, the cost of water provision, on average, exceeds revenues from use (figure 1.5). Of the 20 cities in figure 1.5, only 8 do not recover their operating costs for water supply and sanitation through fees. As a result, India's urban water sector can survive only on large operating subsidies and capital grants from the States.

In sum, excessively low price caps reduce the incentives for infrastructure providers to expand coverage. They also put utilities under financial stress—enough to harm service quality.

The legal and contractual framework

Any pricing rule will be laid down in a legal document. But the commitment value of legal arrangements varies across countries. Investors seeking protection from potentially arbitrary regulators may prefer contracts that are subject to court supervision—or even regulations enshrined in the law, which can be hard to change.[9] Generally, a regulatory regime's most prudent legal form will depend on the quality of the institutions that safeguard and administer it.

Governance challenges

Usually there is a tradeoff between contractual commitment and flexibility (since regulations may require adjustment to unforeseen circumstances). Managing this tradeoff is the key challenge for the designers of a regulatory institution. Typically they seek mechanisms to protect the regulatory body from undue political influence by regulated firms—while giving the regulator some leeway in the application of rules.

A lack of transparency in policy and planning and a lack of quality and integrity in decision making may be called the accountability gap (OECD 2012). This is an issue for both public and private service provision, although the specific characteristics of the issues depend on whether it is public or private service provision. Improved monitoring of outcomes, enhanced use of benchmarking,

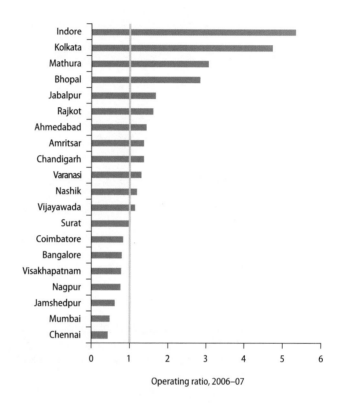

FIGURE 1.5   Utilities in some of India's largest cities do not recover their operating and management costs for water supply and sanitation through user fees, 2006–07

Operating ratio, 2006–07

Source: World Bank.
Note: The operating ratio is the ratio of operating costs, excluding depreciation and debt service, to operating revenues, excluding operating subsidies. A provider's ability to cover all its operating costs (as defined above) through fees (and other nonsubsidy revenue sources) would be reflected in an operating ratio of 1.

and increased public awareness, concern, and involvement could all contribute to better planning and implementation of infrastructure service provision. In addition, for private sector service provision, a transparent process of awards and contract provisions including, as mentioned above, barriers to revise contract provisions ex post are all key components of effective infrastructure provision planning (box 1.2). Key governance challenges include: coordinating the service delivery level and financing decisions, addressing the accountability gap, and coordinating across sectors and space.

The iterative process of setting objectives against available resources in multistake-

BOX 1.2   Successful policy reform in Armenia is based on a well-defined policy framework, clear service-level targets, and incentives for public private participation

In 1995 when a local self-governance system was created in Armenia, the responsibility for water supply and sanitation was delegated to municipalities. But most of them did not have the necessary organizational and financial capacities to manage water supply and sanitation services, especially small municipalities. Systems were in disrepair and despite an abundance of water in the country for almost all Armenians, water was available for only a few hours a day.

In response to these challenges, a policy framework has been created with the support of the World Bank. This includes a revised legal and regulatory framework, the establishment of four water opera-

tors at the regional level, the use of Yerevan Water at the municipal level for 80 percent of the population, public-private participation with increasing private sector involvement and responsibility over time, and the establishment of clear performance targets.

On the whole, the results have been very positive. For example, from 2000 to 2009, the number of hours of water supply in Yerevan increased from 4–6 hours a day to 18–19, and electricity consumption was reduced by more than half.

Contributed by Michael Jacobsen, based on OECD (2011) and World Bank (2011a).

holder policy dialogues coined Strategic Financial Planning by the Organisation for Economic Co-operation and Development (OECD) must be carried out in the context of broader sector and urban planning that addresses the role and responsibility of public agencies, policy priorities, and related regulatory and legislative issues in order to ensure that the result is a package of measures, which can be realistically financed (OECD 2009 and 2011). Efforts to improve the effectiveness of service delivery and lowering of capital costs are needed in most cities. These efforts may be supported by a range of planning tools including strategic financial planning, legislative and regulatory reform, benchmarking, and performance tools and by combining both funding and service provision from the public and private sector (World Bank 2012b).

In most countries, particularly, but not solely, in Africa, there is a dearth of information to guide policy makers and planners. Often there is asymmetry of information across national and local level actors involved in policy and planning. For example, in the water sector, information about basic issues (such as the water supply and sanitation coverage and the source, quality, and timely availability of water consumed by households) is limited at the local level and precious little data are available about the economic and

institutional implications of planning decisions. Sharing information across all levels of government, as well as between sector agencies at one level of government, is indispensable for sound planning. OECD (2012) calls this the information gap. In addition, particularly for water, the geographical mismatch between hydrologic and administrative boundaries is a major obstacle to successful planning. OECD (2012) calls this the administrative gap. Metropolitan areas, with their overlapping jurisdiction and political fragmentation, can lead to incoherent and, at worst, mutually exclusive water management planning and practice. Similarly, the city's dependence on the catchment and competition for water may threaten city-level planning. For example, the water supply of Adelaide, Australia, depends crucially on water uses for irrigation and other purposes higher in the Murray-Darling catchment. Singapore's much touted "four taps" water management strategy aims to reduce the reliance on supply from Malaysia, as heavy reliance on one upstream source is perceived to entail risks (World Bank 2012b).

Establishing subsidies

Public policy can set service prices below cost-recovery levels to meet social and environmental obligations. When prices are set to cover all the costs of an infrastructure project, including the cost of capital, systems will likely be built out to serve all customers who are ready to pay the service cost. But policy makers may also want access to infrastructure to be extended to other customers—both for equity and for environmental sustainability. Price discrimination and subsidies can boost coverage and access.

Social equity

The poor often pay higher prices per unit of, for example, water or energy, than do wealthier people. Water vendors in poor urban areas may charge several times the unit cost of modern water service (Klein 2012). Price discrimination is a way to restore equity by charging rich people more and poor people less.

One method of price discrimination is to offer the poor a specially tailored price-quality mix. For example, poor people who can afford to buy water at times—but not regularly—can do so by the bucket. Or the poor can be served by simpler pipelines. In other ways, too, the poor can be offered flexible service that is better than what they had before, yet not exactly what the rich receive. (Water that is not fully treated can still serve many common uses, such as flushing toilets. Poor people can make their water potable by boiling it.) Finally, the poor can be given more flexible payment terms—for example, through the use of electronic cards. In pursuing these possibilities, it can help to let unconventional providers—from for-profit vendors to community-based organizations—enter the market (Baker 2009). While these are clearly not the only solutions for improving access to water, they provide various second-best options to provide services of varying quality.

Governments can also provide subsidies for equity. However, one must recognize that many subsidies do not increase access to services. For example, subsidizing an existing utility may help the better-off people who are already connected—and no one else (Estache and de Rus 2000; Komives et al. 2005).

Accordingly, city leaders should focus discussions of subsidies on policies to expand access. They should target subsidies to poor people—whether by conducting means-testing (as in Chile's water subsidy system), by targeting areas where the poor tend to live, or by offering lifeline rates (for reduced service at a reduced price). Lifeline rates raise an objection, though: they can benefit people at any income level. Such objections are a reminder that subsidies require careful design. Basing them on quantity or consumption does not necessarily promote equity. A study of 26 quantity-based subsidy cases in Africa, Asia, and Latin America suggested that 24 were regressive, and that where coverage is not universal, connection subsidies may be better at reaching the poor (Komives et al. 2005).

Environmental sustainability

Public transport can mitigate urban congestion: a bus carrying 40 or 50 people takes up no more road space than two or three private cars. And public transport pollutes less, generating fewer greenhouse emissions. Yet in many countries, public transport is unaffordable for the poor.

For example, households in Kampala, Uganda, pay $13 a month on fares, about 8 percent of their budget (World Bank 2011e). Although that is consistent with global estimates of what people pay for transport, it is unaffordable for the poor. To use public transport, the poorest 20 percent of households would need to spend 41 percent of their income on fares. Similar patterns appear in other cities worldwide.

The predictable result is that, in many developing countries, urban public transport ridership is low. In cities where transport fares do not cover the full cost of service provision, transport subsidies can boost ridership. But such subsidies, to succeed, require strong contractual agreements and regulation.

The problem is that even after fares are decoupled from full operating costs, transport providers still need assurance that their costs will be met by revenues. Cities such as Bogotá, Curitiba (Brazil), London, and Seoul have solved the problem with gross cost

FIGURE 1.6   **Public transit fares do not recover operating costs in many of the world's largest cities**

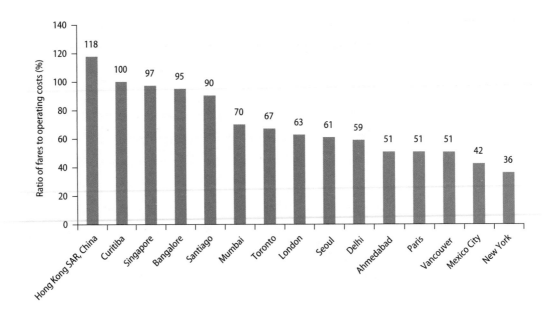

Source: Urbanization Review team.
Note: The numbers in this chart relate to bus and metro systems operated by public entities or large corporate entities. A weighted average was based on ridership across modes. Small private operators were not included because data were lacking.

contracts, which assure operators that their revenues will be based on performance—not on fare box collections (or not directly so). To cover costs fully, public agencies then seek other sources of revenue.

Transport systems around the world vary widely in the share of operating costs that they recover through fares. In a sample of 15 public transit systems, only 2 fully covered their costs through fares. In Paris, 51 percent of costs were recovered through fares; in New York, 36 percent (figure 1.6). While public transport systems appear to be subsidized, what matters for mobility is the relative price of public and private transport. It turns out private transport in many cities worldwide are subsidized—as their full costs are not recognized because road use and parking are not charged efficiently. In Delhi, for example, the relative prices of driving to public transit range between 1.91 and 4.13; in Tokyo, a city with low metro fares and high gasoline prices, the relative prices range between 5.19 and 7.20; in New York, the cost of mass transit is high, but the cost of parking is high, as well, so that the relative price of driving relative to using public transit is as high as Tokyo at 6.75 (World Bank 2011d).

Financing subsidies

Across sectors, subsidies can be funded by various taxes. Or they can be funded through cross-subsidies. In Paris, where fares cover less than 40 percent of public transit operating costs, the main additional revenue source for transport operations is an employment tax levied on employers as a share of their wage bill (see figure 1.6). The tax is justified on the grounds that public transport investments increase the employers' access to labor markets.

For services other than transport, cross-subsidies could require richer urban consumers to pay prices in excess of cost—allowing providers to charge poorer customers less, perhaps in rural areas or in peripheral neighborhoods. (Spotlight B discusses this approach.) But the viability of such cross-sub-sidies varies inversely with the scope for com-petition in the infrastructure sector. Where head-to-head competition exists, high prices in urban areas could attract new entrants to undercut an incumbent who depends on the urban market to cover rural costs through cross-subsidies. In such cases, a better solu-tion is a general tax scheme on all providers. Several telecommunications regimes impose this type of general levy, which is used to fund universal access.

Price discrimination and subsidies can expand access to infrastructure services for equity and for environmental sustainability. Still, city leaders should look first at market structures that give providers the needed incentives and flexibility to cover costs while serving as many people as possible.

Notes

1. In the United States, transaction taxes are around 1–2 percent of property values.
2. Doing Business and Investment Climate Surveys.
3. *Head-to-head competition* refers to the case where firms compete *in the market*. In this kind of competition, firms must offer a price lower than that of their competitors (for a cer-tain quality) in order to increase their profits. This keeps a check on prices. In cases where head-to-head competition is not possible due to the existence of monopolistic characteristics, a competitive market can be mimicked through the use of auctions. This is called *competition for the market*.
4. Networks are said to have "natural monopoly" characteristics. Marginal costs tend to fall for additional connections, making profitable entry into segments of the network infeasible as long as the network monopoly is free to charge any prices it likes.
5. In situations with network externalities, pri-vate underinvestment may justify government intervention to provide infrastructure services (see chapter 2).
6. For state-owned firms, governments may use performance contracts (such as the *contract*-plans traditionally found in France).
7. This doctrine is a fundamental principle in utility regulation, stating that capital assets

must be physically used and useful to ratepay-ers before they can be asked to pay the costs associated with them (Newbery 2001).
8. Other schemes can help build credibility. The German electricity company, RWE, initially escaped nationalization by splitting its prof-its 50–50 with the government. Similarly, resource rents are sometimes shared in min-ing contracts (an example is resource rent taxation).
9. Some call this "regulation by contract" (for example, Gómez-Ibáñez 2003). Not funda-mentally different from other regulatory rules, regulation by contract merely happens to rely (partly) on enforcement by the courts.

References

Annez, Patricia Clarke, and Johannes F. Linn. 2010. "An Agenda for Research on Urban-ization in Developing Countries: A Summary of Findings from a Scoping Exercise." Policy Research Working Paper Series 5476, World Bank, Washington, DC.

Baker, Judy L., ed. 2009. *Opportunities and Chal-lenges for Small Scale Private Service Provid-ers in Electricity and Water Supply: Evidence from Bangladesh, Cambodia, Kenya, and the Philippines.* Washington, DC: World Bank.

Bertaud, Alain. 2004. "Mumbai FSI/FAR Conun-drum: The Perfect Storm: The Four Factors Restricting the Construction of New Floor Space in Mumbai." http://alain-bertaud.com/AB_Files/AB_Mumbai_FSI_conundrum.pdf.

———. 2011. "Hanoi's Urban Structure: Spatial Development Issues and Potential." Report prepared as a background paper for the Viet-nam Urbanization Review.

Bertaud, Alain, and Jan K. Brueckner. 2004. "Analyzing Building-Height Restrictions: Pre-dicted Impacts, Welfare Costs, and a Case Study of Bangalore, India." Policy Research Working Paper 3290, World Bank, Washing-ton, DC.

Cervero, Robert. 1998. *The Transit Metropolis: A Global Inquiry.* Washington, DC: Island Press.

Chamon, Marcos, Paolo Mauro, and Yohei Okawa. 2008. "Mass Car Ownership in the Emerging Market Giants." *Economic Policy* 23 (54): 243–96.

DANE (Departamento Administrativo Nacional de Estadística). 2005. "General Census 2005

(XVII of Population and Dwelling and VI of Housing)." Bogotá.

Doing Business Survey. 2012. http://www.doing business.org/data/exploretopics/registering-property Accessed December 24, 2012.

Dowall, David E. 1992. "A Second Look at the Bangkok Land and Housing Market." *Urban Studies* 29 (1): 25–37.

———. 1998. "Making Urban Land Markets Work: Issues and Policy Options." Prepared for seminar on Strategy on Urban Development and Local Governments, World Bank, Washington, DC.

———. 2012. "Making Cities Work: Planning and Managing Land Use." Background paper for this report.

Estache, Antonio, and Andres Gomez-Lobo. 2004. "The Limits to Competition in Urban Bus Services in Developing Countries." Policy Research Working Paper 3207, World Bank, Washington, DC.

Estache, Antonio, and Ginés de Rus, eds. 2000. *Privatization and Regulation of Transport Infrastructure: Guidelines for Policymakers and Regulators*. WBI Development Studies. Washington, DC: World Bank.

General Statistics Office of Vietnam. 2009. "2009 Population and Housing Census." Hanoi.

Gómez-Ibáñez, José A. 2003. *Regulating Infrastructure: Monopoly, Contracts and Discretion*. Cambridge, MA: Harvard University Press.

Guasch, Jose L. 2004. *Granting and Renegotiating Infrastructure Concession: Doing It Right*. Washington, DC: World Bank.

Hallegatte, Stéphane. 2009. "Strategies to Adapt to an Uncertain Climate Change." *Global Environmental Change* 19 (2): 240–7.

Henderson, J. Vernon, and Hyoung Gun Wang. 2007. "Urbanization and City Growth: The Role of Institutions." *Regional Science and Urban Economics* 37 (3): 283–313.

Hook, Walter. 2005. "Institutional and Regulatory Options for Bus Rapid Transit in Developing Countries: Lessons from International Experience." *Transportation Research Record* 1939: 184–91.

IBGE (Instituto Brasileiro de Geografia e Estatística). 2000. "Demographic Census 2000: Population and Household Characteristics—Universe Results." Rio de Janeiro.

Klein, Michael. 2012. "Infrastructure Policy: Basic Design Options." Policy Research Working Paper 6274 (background paper for this report), World Bank, Washington, DC.

Komives, Kristin, Vivien Foster, Jonathan Halpern, and Quentin Wodon, with support from Roohi Abdullah. 2005. *Water, Electricity, and the Poor—Who Benefits from Utility Subsidies?* Washington, DC: World Bank.

Lei, Qi, and Lu Bin. 2008. "Urban Sprawl: A Case Study of Shenzhen, China." 44th ISOCARP Congress, Dalian, China, September 19–23.

Levy, John. M. 2011. *Contemporary Urban Planning* 9th Ed. Boston, MA: Longman.

Ministry of Home Affairs. 2001. "Census of India: Census Data 2001." Office of The Registrar General and Census Commissioner, New Delhi.

New York City Planning Department. 2011. "Floor Area Ratio Variations across Manhattan." City of New York.

Newbery, David M. 2001. *Privatization, Restructuring, and Regulation of Network Utilities*. Cambridge, MA: Massachusetts Institute of Technology.

OECD (Organisation for Economic Co-operation and Development). 2009. "Strategic Financial Planning for Water Supply and Sanitation." Paris.

———. 2011. "Meeting the Challenge of Financing Water and Sanitation." Paris.

———. 2012. *Meeting the Water Reform Challenge*. Paris: OECD Publishing.

Pelling, Mark. 2003. *The Vulnerability of Cities: Natural Disasters and Social Resilience*. London: Earthscan.

Ruiz, Francisco, and Gabriel Vallejo. 2010. "Using Land Registration as a Tool to Generate Municipal Revenue: Lessons from Bogota." Annual Bank Conference on Land Policy and Administration, World Bank, Washington, DC, April 26–27.

Sandroni, Paulo. 2011. "Urban Value Capture in São Paulo Using a Two-Part Approach: Created Land (Solo Criado) and Sale of Building Rights (Outorga Onerosa do Direito de Construir). An Analysis of the Impact of the Basic Coefficient of Land Use as a Tool of the 2002 Master Plan." Lincoln Institute of Land Policy Working Paper, Cambridge, MA.

Suzuki, Hiroaki, Robert Cervero, and Kanako Iuchi. 2012. *Transforming Cities with Transit: Transit and Land-Use Integration for Sustainable Urban Development*. Washington, DC: World Bank.

PLANNING, CONNECTING, AND FINANCING CITIES—NOW

Uganda Bureau of Statistics. 2010. *Uganda National Household Survey 2009/2010.* Kampala.

Uribe, Maria C. 2010. "Land Information Updating, a De Facto Tax Reform: Bringing Up to Date the Cadastral Database of Bogota." In *Innovations in Land Rights Recognition, Administration and Governance,* ed. Klaus Deininger. Washington, DC: World Bank.

Viguie, Vincent, and Stéphane Hallegatte. 2012. "Trade-Offs and Synergies in Urban Climate Policies." *Nature Climate Change* 2: 334–7.

World Bank. 2002. *World Development Report 2003: Sustainable Development in a Dynamic World.* Washington, DC: World Bank.

———. 2008. *World Development Report 2009: Reshaping Economic Geography.* Washington, DC: World Bank.

———. 2011a. *Europe and Central Asia Knowledge Brief.* December 2011, Volume 44. Washington, DC: World Bank.

———. 2011b. "Indonesia: The Rise of Metropolitan Regions: Increasing the Urban Dividend." Washington, DC: World Bank.

———. 2011c. "São Paulo City Study: Policy Report." São Paulo.

———. 2011d. *The Right Turn: Ensuring Development Through a Low-Carbon Transport Sector.* Washington, DC: World Bank.

———. 2011e. "Planning for Uganda's Urbanization." Inclusive Growth Policy Note 4. World Bank, Washington, DC.

———. 2011f. "Vietnam Urbanization Review." Technical Assistance Report. The World Bank. Washington, DC.

———. 2012a. *Inclusive Green Growth: The Pathway to Sustainable Development.* Washington, DC: World Bank.

———. 2012b. *Integrating Urban Planning and Water Management in Sub-Saharan Africa.* Washington, DC: World Bank.

———. 2013. *Urbanization beyond Municipal Boundaries: Nurturing Metropolitan Economies and Connecting Peri-urban Areas in India.* Directions in Development Series. Washington, DC: World Bank.

Slums are not inevitable: Rules for flexible land use and coordinated connections can improve living conditions

The United Nations projects that 2 billion people will live in slums by 2030. How to manage slum formation and reduce the hazards faced by slum dwellers?[1] Most policy discussions tend to focus on moving people to safe environments or providing better housing elsewhere. Proposed objectives include urban upgrades, such as community and household infrastructure projects; resettlement to new housing developments; housing subsidies; and land titling.

But many of these policies do not work. The reason is that people do not always willingly trade away a better location for a better home with modern utilities. People choose neighborhoods for their affordable services and amenities—but also for their proximity to jobs.

In many developing-country cities, it can be difficult to live near one's job, because land markets have failed: formal housing supply is low, in part because of restrictive regulations. But it may also be difficult and costly to commute to work, because transport infrastructure fails to connect urban neighborhoods. Commuting by public transit in many African cities would cost more than half a poor household's income. In Harare, Zimbabwe, the poor spend more than a fourth of their disposable income on transport (Hook 2005).

Do many people live in slums by choice, simply because the tradeoffs from commuting would be too great? This seems at least possible. What is certain is that many slum dwellers are people for whom even the cheapest public transit would be too expensive. And it is an illustrative fact that in Mumbai more than three in five commuters walk to their jobs.

To foster better living conditions, city leaders can coordinate land market rules with urban infrastructure development. Hanoi has been able to grow without the formation of large slums because the government set prudent rules for land markets and infrastructure. It allowed the densification of former village areas. It pushed for modernizing road networks just outside the city, yet it mostly avoided demolishing older houses. These roads have opened new land for formal developers while improving connections between existing village areas and the city. The village areas were allowed to grow and were integrated into the urban economy.

City leaders in Bogotá similarly succeeded by coordinating land use with infrastructure development. The Programa de

Mejoramiento Integral de Barrios (PMIB) aimed at improving mobility and living conditions in 26 of the poorest city areas, called Unidades de Planificacion Zonal. The Unidades comprised 107 neighborhoods of informal origin, with 1,440 informal settlements, 300,000 plots not formally titled, and about half million structurally substandard dwellings. The PMIB legalized homes and neighborhoods; it expanded infrastructure with roads, rainwater traps, and sanitary and aqueduct trunk networks; and it added urban facilities (stairs, parks, community rooms). Living conditions improved for about 650,000 people.

Other cities, such as Bangkok and Jakarta, still do not consistently coordinate land use with infrastructure. Their undeveloped main roads and transit systems are extremely congested, even though the cities are far less dense than, say, Hanoi. Their housing supply has overtaken their transport infrastructure—making housing fairly cheap, but surrounding it with gridlock. In Jakarta, the loss in productivity is severe.

In cities such as Delhi and Mumbai, housing supply has been restricted by rules preventing the development of land. The outcomes have been very expensive housing, low housing consumption—and often poor mobility, because of infrastructure's failure to adapt.

In still other countries where the rules for land and infrastructure were not set prudently, households ended up disconnected from jobs. The government of South Africa tried to manage costs for subsidized housing by choosing isolated sites, with lower land values, for about two million newly built homes. But there was no plan to connect these subsidized homes to the job market. Many workers now commute in collective taxis, which are slow and expensive. The roads are not good enough to handle traffic

efficiently, and multiple transfers are needed to reach dispersed jobs (Bertaud 2009). Buses carry other workers on commutes that last nearly as long as the work day itself.

Two main lessons emerge from these cities' experiences:

- Efforts to alleviate slum growth and unsafe conditions with improved housing should not have the unintended effect of reducing workers' access to labor markets.
- Setting rules for land and infrastructure coordination can connect generations of workers to jobs—and earn city leaders the right to say that their policies have transformed urban living conditions.

Note

1. Slum dwellers, though not all living in hazard prone areas, are more likely than others to do so. Studies show that the share of the world's urban population subject to natural hazards will more than double by 2050. Today, 370 million people live in cities in earthquake prone areas, 310 million in cities with high probability of tropical cyclones. By 2050, these numbers are also likely to more than double (Lall and Deichmann 2009).

References

Bertaud, Alain. 2009. "Note on Spatial Issues in Urban South Africa." http://alain-bertaud.com/AB_Files/_vti_cnf/AB_Note%20on%20South%20Africa.pdf.

Hook, Walter. 2005. "Institutional and Regulatory Options for Bus Rapid Transit in Developing Countries: Lessons from International Experience." *Transportation Research Record* 1939: 184–91.

Lall, Somik V., and Uwe Deichmann. 2009. "Density and Disasters: Economics of Urban Hazard Risk." Policy Research Working Paper 5161, World Bank, Washington, DC.

The value of market rules for basic services: For expanded coverage and increased efficiency, it's not all about the money

When policy makers consider how to expand infrastructure and improve the provision of basic services, they have a choice. Rather than give first priority to financing, as is often done, they can look at the structure of markets for basic services—and determine what rules will work best.

In particular, policy makers may consider rules for competitive pricing and cost recovery. Indeed, in many cases the expectation of cost recovery through fees will determine the availability of financing.

Consider Colombia. In 1964, only half the residents of Bogotá and other large cities had access to water, electricity, and sanitation. In smaller cities, coverage was even lower. Today, there is nearly universal access in cities of all sizes—a convergence that took more than 40 years (figure SB.1).

How did Colombia expand service coverage? A big part of the answer is that policy reforms allowed fees to nearly cover costs. For example, average residential water fees more than doubled over 1990–2001 (World Bank 2004). With almost 90 percent of households having a metered connection, household consumption was nearly halved. And that, in turn, reduced the need to develop major new infrastructure.

Even with fee increases, water remains fairly affordable in Colombia. The fee structure allows the government to cross-subsidize: richer households and industrial users pay for the poorest consumers. As a result, the average poor household spends less than 5 percent of its income on utility services.

In the electricity sector, Colombia's government changed the rules to increase efficiency—loosening restrictions on market entry and unbundling electricity provision into four categories (generation, transmission, distribution, and commercialization) (Larsen, Pham, and Rama 2004). The policy change succeeded, transforming the electricity market in Colombia and greatly increasing its output. Indeed, the country became a net exporter of electricity, exporting 1.76 terawatt hours to Ecuador in 2005.

Vietnam also increased electricity coverage—rapidly (figure SB.2). In the early 1990s, electricity reached only a small minority of Vietnamese (about 14 percent). Today, it is available to almost everyone (97 percent). Coverage is almost universally equitable: there is little disparity between rural and urban areas, and regional gaps are minor.

What policies led to Vietnam's steep rise in coverage? In 1995, the government created

FIGURE SB.1   **Access to basic services by city size in Colombia, 1964–2005**

a. Electricity   b. Water   c. Sanitation

◆ 1964   ▦ 1993   ▲ 2005

Sources: DANE 1964, 1993, and 2005; Urbanization Review team calculations.

FIGURE SB.2   **Vietnam achieved near to universal electricity coverage in just over 15 years**

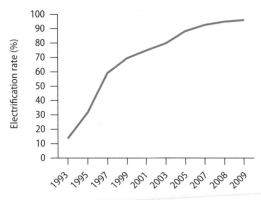

Source: Vietnam General Statistics Office 2009.

a public enterprise, EVN, to manage the electricity system. Prices were kept well below cost, and service expansion was funded by fiscal transfers along with other EVN revenues. But EVN also remained viable by diversifying into other profitable businesses, including telecommunications.

Vietnam's approach has brought benefits to many—but those benefits have come with costs. First, the service is spotty and inefficient, with frequent outages (World Bank 2007). Second, low revenues from electricity provision led EVN to focus on its more profitable ancillary businesses, rather than

on further electricity improvements. Instead of focusing exclusively on universal access, Vietnam's policy makers could have tried to ensure higher quality. It might have been better for all to provide businesses with reliable power than everyone with unreliable service. And Vietnam cannot easily sustain its fiscal support for EVN. The strain on the budget gives the government a stake in seeking alternatives, such as privately financed electricity generation—but those alternatives would require cost recovery through higher fees.

Vietnam's present government is trying to increase electricity fees and attract private financers and generators. It is also considering whether to open the electricity market to competition among generators. Signs indicate that the market can indeed support higher fees (World Bank 2007).

In contrast to Colombia and Vietnam, Uganda still has large gaps in access to basic services throughout the country. In 2008, Uganda's rate of access to improved water sources was 22 percent in urban areas and 5 percent in rural areas (Mugisha and Borisova 2010)—far below the overall average for developing countries (84 percent) and for the Sub-Saharan region (58 percent) (UNDP 2008).

Ugandan policy makers have started thinking about the rules that need to be in place to expand access to basic services. A water reform of 1998 focused on creating the right incentives for more efficient service provision: attributing responsibility to local service managers and increasing their accountability. Since 2000, the national government has been working with the Ugandan National Water and Sewerage Corporation (NWSC)—the autonomous public provider of water and sanitation to the country's large towns—to enforce performance contracts. Renewed every three years, the contracts include specific indicators that NWSC must meet at the end of the period (Banerjee and Morella 2011). However, Uganda's reform has not yet attempted to promote cost recovery through user fees. The NWSC charges a uniform fee across all towns and customer categories served. In 2010, of 23 areas served, only 6 covered production costs.

Policy makers hoping to improve basic services have usually focused on financing. Sometimes they have even expressed objectives as investment targets (such as spending 7 percent of GDP on infrastructure). But the examples of Colombia, Vietnam, and Uganda show the value of rules—three in particular:

- Establish clear and consistent rules for service provision to increase effectiveness, efficiency, and equity.
- Ensure sustainability through full cost recovery from tariffs and/or transfers.
- Where required, subsidize access.

References

Banerjee, Sudeshna G., and Elvira Morella. 2011. *Africa's Water and Sanitation Infrastructure.* Washington, DC: World Bank.

DANE (Departmento Administrativo Nacional de Estadística). 1964. "XIII National Population and II Housing Census." Bogotá.

———. 1993. "XVI National Population and V de Housing Census." Bogotá.

———. 2005. "General Census 2005 (XVII of Population and Dwelling and VI of Housing)." Bogotá.

Larsen, Theo, Huong Lan Pham, and Martin Rama. 2004. "Vietnam's Public Investment Program and Its Impact on Poverty Reduction." World Bank, Hanoi.

Mugisha, Silver, and Tatiana Borisova. 2010. "Development of Pro-poor Water Project in Uganda: A Critical Analysis." *Engineering Economist* 55 (4): 305–27.

UNDP (United Nations Development Programme). 2008. *Assessing Progress in Africa toward the Millennium Development Goals.* New York: United Nations.

Vietnam General Statistics Office. 2009. "Results of the Survey on Household Living Standards 2008." Hanoi.

World Bank. 2004. *Colombia Recent Economic Developments in Infrastructure (REDI). Balancing Social and Productive Needs for Infrastructure.* Washington, DC: World Bank, Finance, Private Sector and Infrastructure Unit, LAC.

———. 2007. "Vietnam Rural Energy Project, Implementation Completion and Results Report." Report ICR485, World Bank, Washington, DC.

2

Connecting cities

A city's connections—external and internal, physical and economic—bear heavily on its future. Where cities and city neighborhoods are disconnected, labor and product markets are not integrated. The results are forgone productivity and higher product prices, costs felt by producers and consumers alike. And as weak connections limit the growth of cities, so feeble cites stunt the growth of countries.

The benefits of strong connections are well understood.[1] Between cities, connections enable firms to access local, regional, and global markets—both for buying inputs and selling outputs. They also give consumers options and, in many cases, better prices. Within cities, connections enable people to access employment; and they enable firms to attract workers, access other inputs, and sell their products in local markets. Enhanced connections can expose cities to new economic opportunities, allowing them to flourish. Policy makers who make markets and jobs more accessible open the door to unforeseen possibilities, facilitating economic transformation.

But city leaders who envision stronger connections for their cities and city neighborhoods face difficult choices. With limited resources, they cannot invest in everything. It is hard to know which new or improved connections will yield the highest returns over time. As facts change, cities will need to adapt. Setting priorities for investment means picking winners and losers in the short run—but in the long run it can make a vast difference for entire cities, even countries. Some decisions lock cities and countries into patterns that last a century or more; others have outcomes that are simply irreversible.

How can policy makers know which connective investments are needed and will yield the highest returns? What related considerations should they keep in mind? To help their cities grow and adapt by identifying the most effective additions and improvements to connective networks, city leaders can take the following three steps:

• Value the city's external and internal connections.
• Coordinate among transport options and with land use, by deciding how to smartly use competition among providers and by balancing cost recovery with targeted subsidies where needed.
• Leverage investments that will yield the highest returns—for one city or for all.

Value the city's external and internal connections

City leaders can value a city's external and internal connections by comparison with other cities—cities in similar countries, cities at similar development stages or urbanization levels, cities with similar per capita income, or cities with similar geographic constraints. Or city leaders can take a more analytical approach, identifying a city's desired connections just as they may identify its desired level of economic specialization or mix of economic activities—through insights from economics and related fields.

Value cities' external connections

How should connections be valued? Physical connections comprise the physical quality and capacity of infrastructure, including road density. Where information on a road network is available, one useful measure is the network's total length. On average, network length is far lower for developing regions than for high-income countries, which contain about 60 percent of the world's paved roads. Even with population size taken into account, the gap remains large.

Measure distances

Where information on road networks is not available, measuring intercity connections becomes a complex task. One cannot simply take the straight-line distance between cities, because this distance fails to account for actual travel conditions in developing countries. Nor is the distance between two

points along a road network a good enough measure, because it ignores bad roads and rough terrain. Rather, the only way to measure connections with reasonable accuracy is to include information on the quality of each network segment. In Malawi, the main road network does not constrain connections very much—but feeder roads do, ratcheting up transport costs. Malawi's primary roads are wide and smooth in comparison with its secondary and tertiary roads, which are narrower, slower, and bumpier (table 2.1).

Again, consider two maps of India—both designed to reveal nationwide variations in market access, but using different measures of the distance between locations (map 2.1, with darker shades indicating lower access). The left panel uses straight-line distance. In contrast, the right panel uses economic distance: a measure designed to account for the number of travel lanes, the roughness of the road, and the pavement ratio. The straight-line distance measure produces much higher access estimates than does the economic distance measure (with transport network conditions considered).

Measure transport costs

In addition to measures of distance, transport costs can be useful for measuring a city's external connections. Typically including direct vehicle operating costs (maintenance, tires, fuel, labor, and capital), transport costs can also incorporate indirect costs (licensing, insurance, road tolls, and roadblock payments).

Measurements of Brazil's annual growth in transport costs for 2009, 2010, and 2011 show that costs have been rising, in real terms, by an average of about 5 percent a year (table 2.2) (World Bank 2011a). Brazil's paved road network, built in the 1950s and 1970s, has since deteriorated (World Bank 2006). Many federal and state roads stand in urgent need of repaving. In 2007, more than 40 percent of roads were considered bad (and less than 35 percent good), a sharp rise from the less than 30 percent that were considered bad in 2000.

Large investments in Brazilian infrastructure are needed. But what investments, and

TABLE 2.1 **Measuring connections along primary, secondary, and tertiary road segments in Malawi**

Road class	Total road length (kilometers)	Number of lanes (average)	International Roughness Index (average)	Pavement ratio (percentage of road surface that is paved)
Primary	1,931.6	1.7	4.4	75.7
Secondary	1,361.0	1.0	6.9	12.9
Tertiary	1,509.2	1.0	6.6	5.5

Source: Lall, Wang, and Munthali 2009.
Note: The International Roughness Index is a comparative measure of road bumpiness.

MAP 2.1 Measuring connections by straight-line distance and by economic distance: Two market-access maps of India

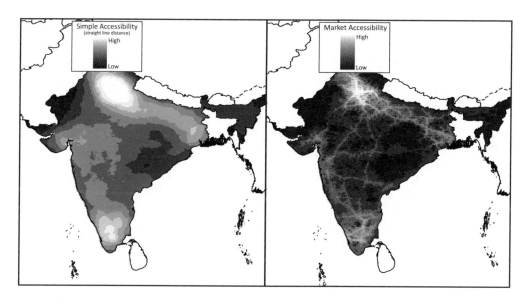

Source: Lall, Shalizi, and Deichmann 2004.
Note: The left heat map is constructed using straight-line distance to measure access, the right heat map using economic distance (incorporating numbers of lanes, International Roughness Index ratings, and pavement ratios). Darker colors indicate lower access.

TABLE 2.2 Brazil's growth in freight transport cost per ton, 2009–11, by distance traveled
(percent)

Distance traveled (kilometers)	2009	2010	2011
6,000	3.73	5.20	5.27
2,400	4.20	5.36	6.09
400	4.56	5.43	7.02
50	4.87	5.54	7.43

Source: Data compiled from Fipe/USP/DECOPE NTC&Logistica.

where? The highest increases in transport costs over the past three years have been over short distances (see table 2.2). Further decomposing the transport costs by source would help explain why they are rising, and why they are rising most on certain road segments. In Vietnam, such decomposition was achieved through a trucking industry survey developed by the World Bank urbanization review team (box 2.1).

Systematically disaggregating transport costs can identify bottlenecks—and reveal

opportunities for infrastructure improvement to yield high dividends. When the trucking survey was administered in India, it showed that transport costs were highest near large cities: a pattern similar to that of Vietnam (and also of Brazil). Freight rates for metropolitan transport in India, defined as trips shorter than 100 kilometers, averaged as high as Rs 5.2 per ton-kilometer ($0.12)—twice the national average of Rs 2.6, and more than five times the cost of such trips in the United States.

Why are India's metropolitan freight transport costs so much higher than its long-haul costs? One reason is the use of smaller, older trucks on metropolitan routes. Another is the higher share of empty backhauls (truckers returning without a load) on metropolitan routes. Finally, trucks on metropolitan routes clock about 25,000 kilometers annually—just a fourth of what they need to be economically viable. To improve coordination and reduce the cost of metropolitan freight movements, trucking firms could adopt logistics

BOX 2.1   Identifying road connection constraints in Vietnam: The World Bank's trucking industry survey

To understand Vietnam's transport infrastructure bottlenecks and reveal the main drivers of its transport costs, the World Bank urbanization review team commissioned a route-specific trucking survey (map B2.1.1). It comprised structured, face-to-face interviews with key managers and owners of trucking companies, as well with individual operators who owned or leased their trucks as independent businesses. The final sample included 246 respondents answering questions on 852 data points (origin-destination combinations).

The survey suggested that corruption and poor road conditions were the main causes of bottlenecks

in Vietnamese truck transport. On average, truck operators rated the severity of corruption at 3.7 out of 5 and the severity of poor road conditions at 3.1 out of 5.

Trips in the vicinity of Hanoi and Ho Chi Minh City appeared to have higher transport costs. About 13 percent of transport costs around Ho Chi Minh City, and 6 percent around Hanoi, consisted of informal facilitation payments (such as bribes). On average, such payments account for about 8 percent of all trucking operation costs.

MAP B2.1.1   **Origin cities in the Vietnam trucking industry survey**

Source: World Bank 2011c.

management systems; they could collaborate or consolidate with competitors; or they could form trucking associations. If India's high freight costs are not reined in, then they—like Vietnam's—will affect national economic development. That is because both nations have large concentrations of economic activity in metropolitan areas.

Transport prices depend partly on the quality and capacity of infrastructure. But they also reflect the governance and market structure of the transport sector, since the indivisibility of transport networks leads to natural monopolies (World Bank 2008). For example, once a rail network is built, other firms are unlikely to enter the market. The fixed costs of building a second network are too high—and the owner of the existing one can bar other providers from it or charge them prohibitive fees for its use. The government therefore needs to promote competitive behavior in transport service provision—but how? One way is to own the network. Another is to regulate prices at competitive levels (Klein 2012).[2]

Value a city's internal connections

In planning to increase access, to ensure affordability, and to keep traffic and pollution within acceptable limits, policy makers need to begin by assessing a city's mobility constraints. A good first step is to look at three measures: transport mode, street density, and population density.

Measure the use of transport modes

First, what is the modal split of commutes to work? In Uganda, data from national surveys suggest that 64 percent of urban workers commute on foot—a figure that rises to 70 percent in Kampala (figure 2.1). For people who live far from a city's economic centers, few jobs are available within walking distance—so the prevalence of foot commuting constrains labor markets. It may also exacerbate slums, as many people will trade away housing quality to be near their jobs. And it points to the insufficiency of affordable transport options (see chapter 1) (Kumar and Barrett 2008).

FIGURE 2.1   How do urban workers commute in Uganda?

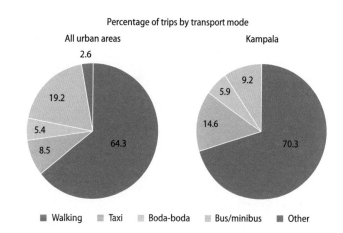

Percentage of trips by transport mode

All urban areas

Kampala

■ Walking   ■ Taxi   ■ Boda-boda   ■ Bus/minibus   ■ Other

Source: Uganda Bureau of Statistics 2010.
Note: A boda-boda is a bicycle taxi.

Measure street density

Second, street density can also help to identify constraints on mobility among a city's neighborhoods. Map 2.2 shows streets wider than 15 meters in the central business districts of Bangkok, Hanoi, New York, and Seoul. They indicate that Hanoi's street density, though greater than Bangkok's, is less than a third of New York's—while Hanoi lacks the transport alternatives of a city such as New York or Seoul (both have extensive underground metro systems).

Measure population density

Third, information on street density can be combined with population size and density to predict the stress that added vehicles would create for road networks. For example, if car ownership in Hanoi were to rise until it equaled the average in Malaysia (250 cars per 1,000 inhabitants), the result—assuming no expansion of road or other transport infrastructure—would be total gridlock in the central part of Hanoi. To ensure that just half of Hanoi's cars could travel at 30 kilometers per hour after the assumed increase in car ownership, Hanoi's vehicular street area would need to rise from 9 percent of the built up area—the present total—to 19 percent. Note that population densities are much

MAP 2.2   **Street densities compared: The central business districts of Bangkok, Hanoi, New York, and Seoul**

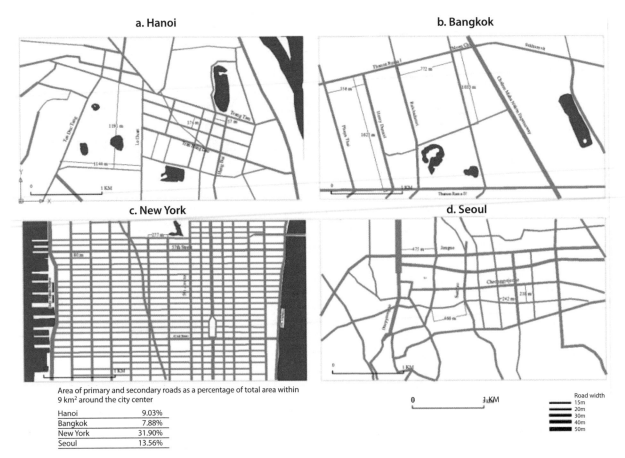

Area of primary and secondary roads as a percentage of total area within 9 km² around the city center

Hanoi	9.03%
Bangkok	7.88%
New York	31.90%
Seoul	13.56%

Source: World Bank 2011c.

higher in Hanoi's central districts (nearly 400 persons per hectare) than across Hanoi (188 persons per hectare) (World Bank 2011c).

Measure transport prices and compare them with transport costs—and consider the benefits of competition

As discussed above, when constraints on a city's external connections are associated with distance, the constraints can be measured using transport costs and physical measures. But many constraints on connections—internal and external alike—are induced by policy.

To measure constraints induced by policy, city leaders can look at transport prices.

Transport prices reflect various factors: transport costs, operator overhead, operator profit, regulatory constraints, and market structure. The last of these—market structure—is a key determinant of prices in the transport industry. As noted above, some transport markets are natural monopolies. Another cause of monopolistic behavior is the emergence of transport scale economies, leading to a vicious circle between higher costs and lower trade and traffic. Areas with high demand and large freight volumes will generate competition, reducing prices—but areas with lower demand will attract only a few providers, who are likely to seek excessive profits.

Connecting sparsely populated rural areas can enable people and firms to move to more productive areas. It can also increase residents' access to schools, health centers, and local markets. However, given that lagging places do not have great market potential (and the volumes transported are likely to be small), it can be hard to attract transport operators to these areas—let alone induce competition among them. Merely improving roads or deregulating the market will not suffice. In these cases, policy makers can encourage intermediate modes of transport. Bicycles, hand carts, motorcycles, power tillers and trailers, and community participation—all can increase mobility in rural areas (Lall, Wang, and Munthali 2009).

Competition in the market and for the market

Considerable benefits follow from inducing competition in the transport sector. One is greater efficiency. Another is more affordable service. In contrast, a monopolistic sector is likely to be inefficient and unaffordable—and to encourage opportunistic behavior, inviting markups and creating incentives for bribes.

Along major transport routes in Africa, considerable gaps separate transport prices from transport costs (figure 2.2). A recent study by the World Bank suggests that the causes of these gaps are bribes, regulatory rents, and high profits (Teravaninthorn and Raballand 2009). Inefficiencies in logistics, such as large numbers of empty backhauls, could also be driving prices up.

A competitive market brings benefits, not only within transport modes (competition in the market), but also between them (competition for the market). Competition between modes can lower prices, and it can promote the most efficient distribution of transport services for various product types. Generally, most road transport is dominated by short-haul freight—but as distance increases, rail transport becomes more attractive. In India, road transport is estimated to be the least expensive option for distances up to 400 kilometers. Rail prices are lower for distances of 400–700 kilometers. Beyond 700 kilometers, waterways are cheapest (McKinsey & Company 2010). These break points may vary by country, as they depend on truck, train, and

FIGURE 2.2   Gaps between transport prices and costs in Africa suggest a monopolistic transport sector

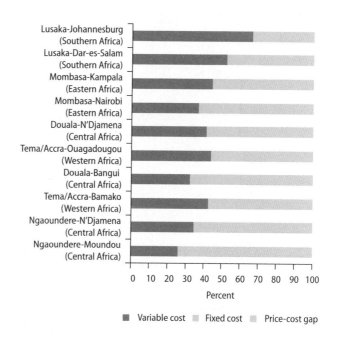

Source: Teravaninthorn and Raballand 2009.

vessel size and on the type of product being transported. Similarly, topographical endowments and barriers are likely to affect the break points.

High demand can have two opposed effects on transport prices. As discussed above, it can attract competition leading to lower prices. But it can also lead to congestion, and congestion—beyond what the infrastructure and its maintenance regimes can readily handle—imposes economic costs. In Sri Lanka, estimates suggest that traffic volumes and poor road maintenance contribute costs equivalent to about 1 percent of GDP (World Bank 2004). And in Colombia, delays in ports (especially the busiest ones) significantly increase transport costs: for every hour that cargo remains idle, the added cost per ton is 826 pesos ($0.69) (Samad, Lozano-Gracia, and Panman 2012). A 2007 study of logistics costs for trucking in Colombia's port terminals showed that, on average, drivers reported nine hours of lag time between joining the queue for entry into port facilities and departing the facilities with a new freight load (Egis Bceom International 2007).

Coordinate among transport options and with land use to improve a city's internal connections

Once city leaders have identified constraints on a city's internal connections, they can determine what is needed for a good transport system—one that connects the city's neighborhoods to each other, giving people a wider choice of places to live and work.

Connections among neighborhoods are a growing problem for cities in developing countries. As incomes rise and populations explode, private motor vehicles strain road capacity. In 1981–2001, for example, while the population of India's six largest metropolitan cities nearly doubled, the number of private motor vehicles increased eightfold. In Delhi alone, motor vehicles shot up from 3.9 million to 5.6 million between 2002–03 and 2007–08. Meanwhile the city's total road length merely crept up, from 30,698 kilometers to 30,985. Because of this disconnection between urban growth and urban infrastructure, trips in large Indian cities are barely faster by car or truck than by bicycle.[3]

Although some urban congestion can be efficient, too much is the opposite. It keeps people stuck in traffic for long hours, unable to reach their jobs—not to mention the health problems caused by pollution. A good transport system allows people to reach jobs while further linking them to education, health, and recreation. Policy makers need ways to boost mobility within a city while managing congestion and pollution, and they need to ensure that transport is available to the poor.

To connect neighborhoods for all these purposes, city leaders can systematically coordinate urban mobility plans with land use policies and related infrastructure plans. In addition, they can seek ways to reduce transport prices—within cities as well as between them—by inducing competition in

transport markets. Finally, they can consider how to balance the aim of covering transport costs through prices against other social and ecological objectives.

Establish a basis for increased mobility within cities

As city leaders seek to improve connections among neighborhoods, they must carefully steer away from options that lock the city into undesirable forms. The best way to avoid such wrong turns is to begin by integrating land use policies with plans for urban mobility.

Integrate land use planning and mobility planning

Plans to connect neighborhoods are inseparable from plans for urban land use—especially density plans. For any of these policies to benefit the city as intended, they must be integrated throughout the planning process. However, urban transport is often an "institutional orphan," with its responsibility often fragmented across agencies. Land use planning is a core function of development authorities, with transport planning often limited to developing the road network. Such fragmentation of responsibilities results in inefficiencies. In Bangalore, India, a new airport, several miles outside the city, was close to being commissioned when city authorities realized that the road connecting the city to the airport was inadequate.

Land use planning is integral to transport planning, because land use will largely determine transport demand. Different cities need different modal mixes, different neighborhoods different modes. Mass transport generally suits compact areas, private vehicles more sprawling ones. Mixed-use plans can reduce the need for long trips by locating housing, shops, services, and jobs all within a short radius. Studies also suggest that higher densities are good for efficiency and for environmental sustainability, reducing energy consumption and emissions by reducing vehicle miles traveled (Newman and Kenworthy

1989; Mokhtarian, Bagley, and Salomon 1998; Schrank, Lomax, and Eisele 2011).

Transport plans, in turn, shape land use by making specific sites more accessible. For example, a new road to undeveloped land can enable its development. Or a new downtown metro connection can boost demand for redevelopment of the urban core.

Look for prudent ways to make transport markets competitive

Not all modes and routes will support multiple transport providers. But where they will—and where demand is high enough—policies and regulations should foster competition and avert monopolies. Competitive pricing can also be encouraged by promoting multiple modes of transport.

Although competition across modes may be desirable, free entry to some individual modes may not be. In bus transport, for example, competition that is excessively fierce—or not structured carefully by planners—can put passengers' lives at risk (see the discussion of Bogotá in chapter 1).

Balance the aim of covering transport costs through market pricing with the complementary objectives of efficiency, equity, and environmental sustainability

Cost recovery through prices need not always mean that transport users pay the whole cost of transport. Urban transport subsidies are sometimes desirable, not only for equity and the environment (reducing emissions and so forth), but also for efficiency (Gwilliam 1987). For example, subsidies that target lower-income groups to make urban transit more affordable can boost ridership and reduce congestion.

Many cities in the developing world lack affordable transport for their poorest residents. An extreme example is Mumbai, ranked as the 6th most expensive among 27 cities worldwide (Carruthers, Dick, and Saurkar 2005). According to a study published in 2007, for riders in the lowest income category in Mumbai, transport expenditure represented at least 16 percent

of income—even with subsidies covering as much as 30 percent of transport costs (Cropper and Bhattacharya 2007).

Targeted subsidies have not always been successful. But some targeted subsidies reach the right groups and increase their access to jobs. For example, South Africa uses highly subsidized weekly coupons—each for 10 journeys between black townships and industrial development areas—to connect low-income groups to jobs. And Brazil requires formal sector employers to provide transit tickets to their employees through a system called *vale transporte* (transportation voucher, VT); the firms then deduct the VT expenditures from taxable income. The VT system—albeit affecting only the formal sector—effectively spreads the cost of transport subsidies between employers and the government (Gwilliam 2011).

Increase the supply of transport while managing demand and harmful externalities

Once the basis for a better transport system is in place, an urban mobility plan can be made that:

- Increases transport supply (capacity) through new investments and ensures adequate maintenance.
- Improves existing transport systems by managing demand.
- Controls congestion and limits pollution with fiscal and regulatory instruments.

The ultimate objective is to increase the supply of affordable transport options while keeping traffic and pollution within acceptable limits.

City leaders can make investments in added network capacity and multiple transport modes. They can manage the demand for transport through regulation, enacting policies that reduce pressure on existing infrastructure. Finally, they can control traffic and limit emissions with fiscal and regulatory instruments such as subsidies and taxes.

Increase transport supply through new investments, with attention to demand

Because transport infrastructure investments are part of a city's mobility plan, they need to be integrated with its land use plan (as emphasized above). The next section of this chapter—on identifying the investments that will yield the highest returns—presents a detailed discussion of ways to enhance transport supply, between cities as well as within them.

What needs underlining here is that developing cities cannot attain desirable forms unless investments in infrastructure are coordinated with land use—and with efforts to manage demand.

Improve existing transport systems by managing demand

To have strong internal connections, a city must have a transport system that is responsive to demand: not just new roads or a new metro line, but also regulatory and fiscal instruments that will manage the demand for both new and existing infrastructure. This need to manage demand is seldom considered by developing cities—they have traditionally focused on increasing supply (Gómez-Ibáñez 2011).[4]

The management of infrastructure can direct demand to transport modes with unused capacity—relieving pressure on modes that are already congested to the point of strain. It can restrain the demand for travel, or it can incline demand to take a certain form. For example, demand restraint measures can seek to shift commuters from private vehicles to mass transport. They can motivate people to travel during off-peak times. They can seek to reduce trip lengths. And in some cases, they can be designed to render travel unnecessary.

In addition to managing demand, regulations can promote competition in the market or set prices near competitive levels (chapter 1). And they can include policies to mitigate harmful externalities, such as congestion and pollution from vehicle emissions.

Congestion and pollution need to be managed with fiscal and regulatory instruments.

Even with coordination between investments to increase supply and policies to manage demand, individual actions often impose social costs. In transport, these harmful externalities arise mostly from congestion and from pollution (including greenhouse gas emissions).

In the developing world, rapid increases in private motor vehicle use have created excessive congestion. A look at the numbers for Vietnam shows how quickly vehicles have multiplied in recent years (figure 2.3). A recent study estimates the economic costs of traffic congestion to be equivalent to 0.7 percent of GDP in Manila, 0.9 percent in Jakarta, 1.8 percent in Kuala Lumpur, and 2.1 percent in Bangkok (ESCAP 2007).

City leaders often consider building more roads to accommodate rising numbers of private vehicles—yet road expansion in the long run may only attract more vehicles to the road, with no resulting reduction in traffic. Even if congestion declines, fuel consumption and emissions will not. Moreover, new infrastructure requires land and rights-of-way that can be costly and difficult to assemble in cities.

Fiscal and regulatory instruments are another way to manage congestion and limit pollution. Used in combination with infrastructure investments, such instruments can guarantee that the benefits of increased access exceed its social costs. To determine the best instrument in a given case, a cost-benefit analysis can be conducted, with attention to impacts on efficiency, equity, and affordability.

To bring congestion down to manageable levels, policies can discourage the use of personal motor vehicles, making their use more difficult and costly. Measures that have been used include restrictions on available parking space, parking fees that reflect the full economic cost of motorized travel, and a congestion fee for driving in core city areas at peak times.

Congestion fees would seem to be the most efficient instrument for their purpose, as they attack the externality directly. In practice, their use is limited—they tend to be politically costly. Examples in the developed world include London, Singapore, and Stockholm.

The City of London raised £137 million in 2007 from its congestion fees, which by law are reinvested into public transport systems in the city. Drivers entering, leaving, or driving in the congestion zone between 7 a.m. and 6 p.m. on weekdays must pay a fee of about $16 by midnight of the same day. If they do not pay the fee by the next day, it increases to $20. If still unpaid, the fee rises to $240 on the following day and to $360 after 28 days. After that the authorities can tow the car or immobilize it with wheel boots, either action burdening the car owner with $140–$400 in added costs. Residents of the congestion zone must pay, but at a 90 percent discount. Exemptions are given for disabled drivers and for bicycles, motorcycles, and electric or alternatively fueled cars.[5]

London's congestion fee has reduced the number of cars on the roads each day, and it has raised revenue for the city. It is also associated with a 6 percent increase in the number of bus passengers during charging hours. The policy, however, achieves less than it could in two ways. First, drivers have no incentive to limit driving once inside the congestion zone. Second, there is no additional incentive to reduce driving during peak hours, since the fee is constant throughout the day (Litman 2006).

Other cities have tried to discourage the use of cars by making cars expensive to own. They may charge high vehicle taxes or registration fees—or they may hold auctions for the legal right to buy a car. Vehicle taxes have been imposed in Denmark, France, Germany, Malaysia, the Netherlands, Philippines, Sweden, Thailand, and the United Kingdom. Such taxes can be based on engine model and capacity, fuel economy, emissions, weight, or fuel type (Timilsina and Dulal 2010). Auctions are used in Singapore, which since 1990 has limited the annual rise in the vehicle population to 3 percent (a figure reached through long-term projections of land use and transport facility development). The government releases monthly quotas to allocate new

FIGURE 2.3   **The rise of private motor vehicles in Vietnam, 1997–2009**

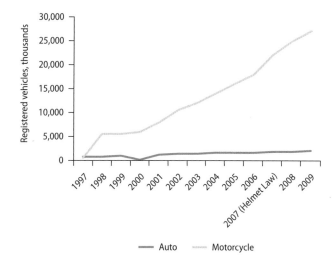

Source: Vietnam's Ministry of Transport.

vehicles, and it issues certificates of entitlement—the right to buy cars—to the highest bidders. Good for 10 years, the certificates can then be renewed at the prevailing permit price (Menon 2002).

Fuel taxes can reduce both congestion and pollution—but they can cause unintended harm if not properly defined. For example, increased transport costs can make products less competitive. One solution to this problem is a discriminatory tax, imposed only on fuels used for private transport (Timilsina and Dulal 2010).

Parking fees can help to manage congestion by shifting travelers from private cars to mass transit. In Ottawa, the reduction of a parking subsidy for government employees from 100 percent of the cost to 30 percent led—one year later—to a 20 percent reduction in employees' trips by private car and a 17 percent increase in their use of public transit (Timilsina and Dulal 2010).

Such fiscal or regulatory instruments are more likely to succeed in combination than alone. When they are designed to shift travelers from one transport mode to another, the other modes must be ready for use, or the instruments will not work as desired.

FIGURE 2.4   **Road fatalities in high-, middle-, and low-income countries, 2003–07**

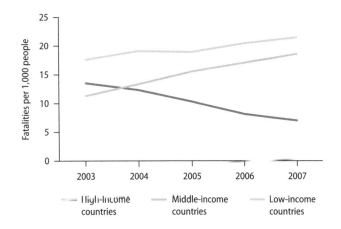

Source: Kopits and Cropper 2003.

Besides congestion, another harmful externality associated with urban transport is unsafe road conditions. Road accidents are one of the largest causes of death worldwide, resulting in 1.2 million annual fatalities. Each hour, about 40 people younger than 25 are estimated to die in crashes.

The poor and vulnerable tend to be the most affected by road accidents. The number of annual road fatalities per 1,000,000 people has risen in low-income countries, even while declining in high-income countries (figure 2.4). Although low- and middle-income countries have only 48 percent of the world's registered motor vehicles, they account for 90 percent of road fatalities. To realize the benefits of stronger connections within cities, regulation to control speeds—and guarantee the safety of public transport—may be essential.

Taxes, standards, and subsidies can also be used to manage pollution and to make transport more affordable. In many cities, the transport sector is the main contributor to local air pollution and greenhouse gas emissions. In Brazil's largest cities, private transportation is the main source of vehicle emissions, even though it is used by just 30 percent of commuters (figure 2.5). Across all city sizes private transportation generates more than 40 percent of greenhouse gas

emissions—and in medium-size cities, those of 100,000–250,000 people, it generates more than 70 percent.

To limit or reduce air pollution and greenhouse gas emissions, city leaders may consider emissions standards a useful instrument. Other measures include pollution taxes, fuel economy standards, and fuel quality standards. Motor vehicle emissions have been regulated since the 1960s and 1970s in Europe and the United States. More recent, new cars have been required to meet emissions standards in Argentina, Brazil, Chile, China, Colombia, India, and Indonesia (following U.S. and European practice). In 2009, California and the European Union set specific standards for carbon dioxide emissions. But fuel economy standards, which also control carbon dioxide, had been established much earlier (in 1975) by the U.S. federal government (Gómez-Ibáñez 2011).

Adding congestion taxes or fuel taxes can further reduce pollution along with congestion. Again, a combination of instruments can be more successful than one—if all are planned within a single framework.

Subsidies may be appropriate for transport modes that are preferable because they are more ecologically sustainable. For example, Mexico City's system for bus rapid transit (BRT) is expected to reduce carbon monoxide emissions by 0.28 metric tons and to generate $3 million each year in health benefits from reduced air pollution. And the Trans-Milenio BRT system in Bogotá, in its first 30 years of operation, will reduce carbon monoxide emissions by an estimated 15 percent, reduce traffic fatalities by 93 percent across the system, reduce local air pollutants by 40 percent, and improve travel time by 32 percent, compared with the transport system that would be available otherwise (Lee 2003; Gómez-Ibáñez 2011).

Because the costs of air pollution are not internalized by private agents, city leaders may choose to subsidize cleaner transport—such as BRT—as a way of internalizing the additional benefits from switching to cleaner modes. Where congestion costs at peak hours are high, policy makers may consider

FIGURE 2.5   **Private transportation is the largest source of vehicle emissions in Brazilian cities, 2009**

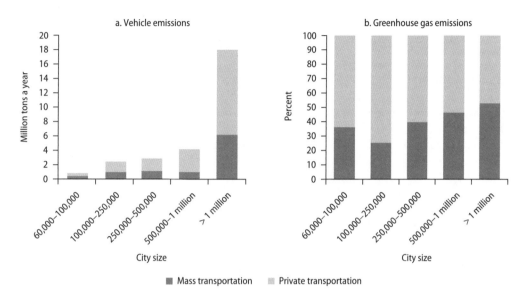

Sources: Associação Nacional de Transportes Públicos; authors' calculations.

demand-side subsidies to shift demand for private cars toward public transit. Subsidizing cleaner vehicles and cleaner fuels can help in reducing pollution and emissions from vehicles, though not in reducing congestion.

Leverage investments that will yield the highest returns

When deciding where and how to improve transport networks, city leaders should identify the most efficient investments in connections throughout a country. Where is demand highest for the expansion of infrastructure and transport services? Which corridors are identified by spatial tools and simulations as most central to the network, in that improving them will yield the highest returns—both locally and nationally, for efficiency and for equity?[6]

Within urban areas, investments to improve connections similarly require integration with long-term planning—especially land use and density plans, as the preceding sections have emphasized. Most cities will benefit from mass transit and from multiple

transport modes. The questions that city leaders must answer concern the particular mix of modes, their specific design, and their integration in the larger urban transport system.

Consider ways to induce healthy competition

More than building and fixing, efforts to improve intercity connections are also about the economics of the transport sector. If the market structure for transport service provision does not promote competitive pricing, any cost reductions stemming from network investments will be absorbed by monopolistic providers as profit. That is because of the sector's tendency toward natural monopolies, discussed earlier in this chapter.

Investments in infrastructure are more successful when bundled with regulatory reforms that promote competitive pricing while ensuring compliance with safety standards. The government regulates in large part to induce healthy competition—limiting monopolistic behavior but also limiting the number or behavior of competitors where required.

In Uganda, as in many other African countries, a large gap between transport costs and prices attests to monopolistic behavior (see figure 2.2). Along the Kampala–Mombasa corridor, home to most of Uganda's industrial production, transport prices are $2.22 per kilometer—double the average price in the United States—even though transport costs per kilometer are about $0.35 per kilometer. According to trucker surveys, 86 percent of the corridor is in good condition. So the fact that providers are making more than 85 percent profit suggests a need for competition, competition that can be most effectively induced through policy measures and regulation (World Bank 2012b).

Use spatial analysis to set priorities for intercity connections

Once the basis for competitive pricing is in place, spatial or geographic analysis can reveal the emerging demand for particular cities and help city leaders identify the investments that will most reduce transport costs. Some spatial tools examine the growth of cities by looking at their demographic and economic footprints. Others point to areas of urban expansion, those where investments can yield the highest returns. Combining this information with data on households and on industry location can suggest where demand is highest for expanded infrastructure or related services (box 2.2).

Transport markets display network externalities, meaning that improvements to one segment can affect the whole network. Spatial tools can help identify the network improvements that will bring the highest positive externalities. And that, in turn, can help city leaders identify and understand the complex tradeoffs between efficiency and equity in decisions about transport infrastructure.

Take Sri Lanka, where transport costs are high by international standards. It costs $2.90 per kilometer to move products there, more than twice the U.S. cost of $1.25. The quality of the road network seems to be a main driver of transport costs: more than half reportedly is in bad condition (World Bank 2010). In deciding which segments to improve, policy makers must weigh two conflicting objectives:

- *Efficiency.* Resources can be allocated to investments that make the most of national income (connecting regions with the highest rate of return), or to those that would reduce transport costs by the greatest amount (compared with investments in other network segments).
- *Equity.* Resources can be distributed equally throughout the country, with no eye to efficiency.

Recent research used a simulation model to measure transport cost savings from alternative infrastructure investments in Sri

---

BOX 2.2   The Republic of Korea's strategic decisions to expand infrastructure networks enabled the development of new towns

City leaders in the Republic of Korea integrated their transport infrastructure investments to enable the spatial evolution of the economy. Figures B2.2.1–B2.2.3 depict changes in the spatial distribution of city sizes, in the share of manufacturing employment, and in proximity to intercity highways. As the left panel in each figure illustrates, in the 1960s the population was concentrated in the cities of Seoul and Busan. The middle panels show how in the 1980s, as these cities grew and manufacturing

was concentrated in and near them, the government made efforts to connect them—to each other and to domestic and international markets. Finally, the right panel in each figure shows how urbanization advanced and large urban centers arose outside Seoul and Busan. Korean manufacturing now remains highly concentrated in and around these two cities—yet government efforts have ensured that the entire national network of cities is well connected.

(box continues on next page)

BOX 2.2   The Republic of Korea's strategic decisions to expand infrastructure networks enabled the development of new towns

FIGURE B2.2.1   As population growth has expanded beyond Seoul and Busan, 1960–2005 . . .

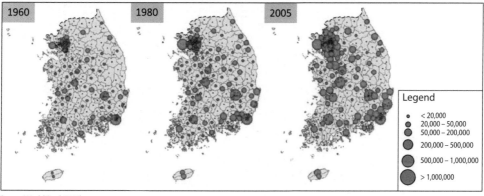

Source: World Bank 2011b.

FIGURE B2.2.2   . . . manufacturing jobs have deconcentrated to secondary cities, 1960–2005 . . .

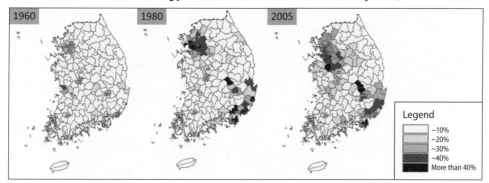

Source: World Bank 2011b.

FIGURE B2.2.3   . . . enabled by improvements in transport connectivity, 1970–2010

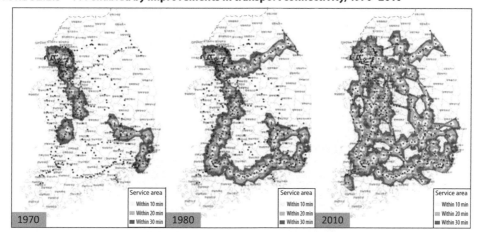

Source: World Bank 2011b.
Note: Journey time to the closest expressway interchange (within 10, 20, and 30 minutes).

MAP 2.3   Connecting mountains of poverty to peaks of prosperity: A spatial tool for comparing transport investments in Sri Lanka

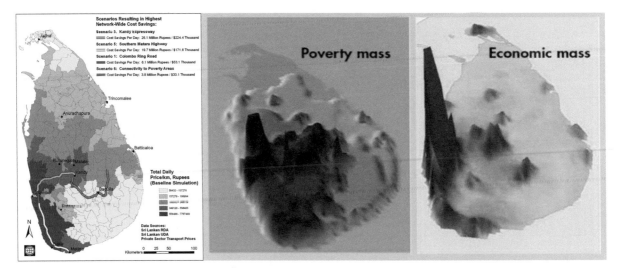

Source: World Bank 2010.

Lanka (World Bank 2010). The main finding: connections in poor and remote areas can be most enhanced by improving roads and transport in areas of intermediate wealth—not in the poorest and most remote areas themselves, where traffic is thin. Improving corridors with the highest potential, such as that from Kandy to Colombo, will connect the most poor people to large markets (map 2.3). Since these investments will promote both efficiency and equity, it makes sense to give them priority.

Similarly, a recent study identified key infrastructure investments for Mozambique using population distribution data and information about the road network (including quality characteristics). The study showed that investments in the five major international transport corridors (in the north of the country), and in the Maputo–Pemba corridor, would greatly reduce travel times between major cities—but would scarcely improve most people's access to markets. Instead, large investments in feeder roads were revealed as the best way to improve connections for people in remote northern areas. If the corridors were paved and kept in good condition while the entire rural road network

was upgraded to high-quality gravel, 9 of 10 people would reside within five hours of a city with at least 50,000 inhabitants (Dorosh and Schmidt 2008).

Increase urban transport capacity—but how?

Discussions of urban transport have traditionally focused on supply. Enhancement was long taken to mean increasing the system's carrying capacity to meet growing demand. Making roads wider, enabling them to hold more traffic, was considered the best approach. But now that rising incomes are making private vehicles more common, adding road space only attracts more cars onto the roads. In place of wider roads, affordable mass transit—either public or private—has come to be seen as a central need for cities.

Why affordable mass transit is essential for urban development in many cities

When urban transport is available and affordable, people are freer to settle in areas across the city. When it is not, people are less free in their choice of housing, locations, and amenities because they are constrained by the need to stay near their jobs. A symptom of this constraint is a large informal market for land and housing—often located precariously on hilltops, floodplains, and the like. In India, data from the 2001 census suggested that slum dwellers were more likely than others to walk or bicycle to work (figure 2.6). Slum dwellers may thus be internalizing the transport constraint as a constraint on location and housing, trading off decent living conditions for the ability to commute and participate in labor markets.

Density and mass transit options

Mass transit can take many forms, including public buses, rail, and BRT. As this chapter has repeatedly indicated, linking transport modes to urban density plans is a critical part of planning infrastructure investments.

A scatter chart of some 30 cities, plotting each city according to its density and its physical concentration around an urban center, shows a consistent pattern: dense and compact cities form a group that emphasizes mass transit, while sparse and sprawling ones

FIGURE 2.6   Foot and bicycle commuting as a share of all commuting, by city

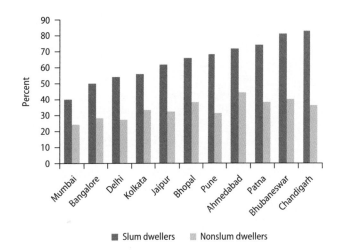

Source: Ministry of Home Affairs 2001.

form a group that relies on private motor vehicles (figure 2.7). Between these two groups is a third, larger group that benefits most by combining the two—indeed, by

FIGURE 2.7   A city's chosen mix of transport modes reflects its spatial structure

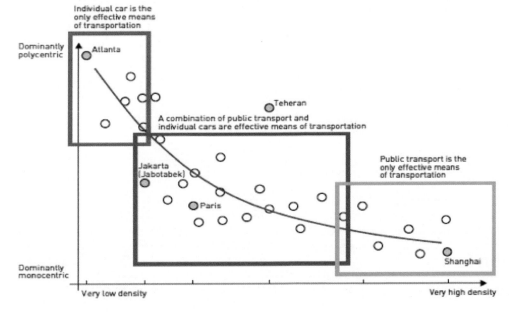

Source: Bertaud and Malpezzi 2003.

integrating several transport modes within a single framework.

Two pivotal choices for transit

Should mass transit use rail or buses? How should various transport modes be integrated within the urban transport system? These are two of the main questions that confront urban mass transit planners.

First: In weighing rail against buses, policy makers should consider that rail transit systems rarely cover operating costs with fares.[7] By comparison, BRT generally requires a lower capital investment—it often uses existing infrastructure, and it runs at ground level (box 2.3). And BRT can operate without subsidies while charging affordable fares, imposing less financial stress on cities (Gwilliam 2011). Note, however, that rail transit's

unrecovered financial cost can be matched or exceeded by its social benefits.

Second, and more important: An essential part of integrating land use and infrastructure planning is the integration of various transport infrastructures within the larger urban mobility plan. Research has suggested that two kinds of integration are needed: physical integration for transfers between modes, and fare integration for avoiding excessive price competition among modes (NEA Transport Research and Training 2003). Further, different modes have also different energy needs, and therefore much can be gained from planning a transport system that integrates the different infrastructures and considers all costs (World Bank 2012a). See spotlight C for country lessons on city placement, policy, and infrastructure.

BOX 2.3   Bus rapid transit: Successful if handled with care

Bus rapid transit (BRT) systems have been praised—including by the World Bank—for their performance capability, their low build cost compared with rail and metro systems, and their ability to operate with small subsidies or no subsidies. Famous projects in Bogotá and Brazil's Curitiba are often touted as BRT successes.

Less often noticed have been the pitfalls and shortcomings of these and other BRT projects. A World Bank review reveals key determinants of success along with certain challenges:

- *Bureaucracy was circumvented.* In all 11 cities studied, planning and implementation teams were formed outside existing public structures to avoid bureaucratic obstructions.
- *Political leadership was on board.* Projects went forward rapidly in cities where the mayor or other political leaders had a clear vision for BRT, such as in Bogotá, Curitiba, Jakarta, and Ecuador's Guayaquil. Projects were stalled, sometimes for years, in cities where no such political commitment was present.
- *Lead times were reduced to match political timetables—but this produced gaps in planning.* Steps

toward project completion were hastened so that elected officials could claim credit before the end of their terms in office. As a result, crucial institutional, legal, and financial issues were sometimes neglected—though BRT planners gave long thought to busway designs (median or curbside), platform types (high or low), fuel technologies (diesel or compressed natural gas), and fare collection mechanisms (on board or prepaid).

- *Fares were defined by political authorities*—sometimes without a complete calculation of costs and revenues.
- *The public was not adequately educated about route changes.* Communication failures occurred in Bogotá, Santiago, Mexico City, and Mexico's León during the expansion of its system—leading to chaotic conditions and, in some cases, dramatic public protests.
- *Existing transport operators protested when their interests were sidelined.* For example, they were not involved in the BRT process through direct negotiations—or the bidding process failed to satisfy them.
- *Fare collection systems were not integrated everywhere with public transit systems.* Such

BOX 2.3   (continued)

disconnections occurred in Beijing, Bogotá, and Mexico City. Even BRT corridors were not always integrated with each other: examples include Jakarta and Quito.

- *Bus scheduling has sometimes led to overuse at peak hours and underuse at off-peak hours.* Peak hour crowding and off-peak inactivity are perhaps the most visible weakness in BRT operation. One or both can be seen in Beijing, Bogotá, Curitiba,

Guayaquil, Jakarta, León, Mexico City, and Quito.

In short, BRT projects indeed have great potential—but they must be carefully planned and carried out.

Sources: Hidalgo, Custodio, and Graftieaux 2007; ITDP 2007.

Notes

1. A vast literature shows positive links between market access and the growth of cities (see, among others, Beeson, DeJong, and Troesken 2001; Henderson and Thisse 2004; and Tao, Hewings, and Donaghy 2010). For example, research on Brazil shows that a 1 percent increase in market potential leads to an increase in city size of 2.7 percent, while a reduction in transport costs of 10 percent leads to a 1 percent increase in city growth over a decade (Da Mata and others 2007).
2. Research on the effects of transport deregulation is a major area in recent transport economics. Much of the impetus for this development has come from outside traditional transport economics, being intellectually stimulated by work in such areas as regulatory capture (Stigler 1971), market structures (Baumol, Panzar, and Willig 1982), and new regulatory instruments (Laffont 1994).
3. Bicycles are typically ridden at around 15 kilometers per hour.
4. For example, the Ho Chi Minh City plan for 2025 contains a proposal to build a 161-kilometer rail system and highway investments of more than $9.8 billion.
5. Transport for London/Congestion Charging. www.tfl.gov.uk/roadusers/congestioncharging, accessed September 28, 2010.
6. In the transport sector, network economies—where the benefits from connecting two points extend to all related connections in the network—can often benefit from policy measures

(Economides 1996). That is because a private agent whose interests span only two points in the network might not realize the wider benefits of connecting them. Say that a new road connects Hanoi and Guangzhou. With this link, a firm in Hanoi has expanded its output market by the total number of additional cities that can be reached through Guangzhou. Furthermore, because Ho Chi Minh City is already connected to Hanoi and Guangzhou to Beijing, the new road lets firms in Ho Chi Minh City sell in Beijing. Ignoring such network effects can lead to underinvestment in infrastructure connections.
7. Few cities can bring the cost of rail transit close to the revenues from rail transit. Those few cities share three important characteristics: they are large in absolute terms, they have highly concentrated corridor flows, and they have medium to high incomes that warrant fairly high revenues per passenger (Gwilliam 2011).

References

Baumol, William J., John C. Panzar, and Robert D. Willig. 1982. *Contestable Markets and the Theory of Industry Structure.* San Diego, CA: Harcourt Brace Jovanovich.

Beeson, Patricia E., David N. DeJong, and Werner Troesken. 2001. "Population Growth in U.S. Counties, 1840–1990." *Regional Science and Urban Economics* 31: 669–99.

Bertaud, Alain, and Stephen Malpezzi. 2003. "The Spatial Distribution of Population in

48 World Cities: Implications for Economies in Transition." http://alain-bertaud.com/AB_Files/Spatia_%20Distribution_of_Pop_%2050_%20Cities.pdf.

Carruthers, Robin, Malise Dick, and Anuja Saurkar. 2005. *Affordability of Public Transport in Developing Countries*. Transport Papers 3. Washington, DC: World Bank.

Cropper, Maureen, and Soma Bhattacharya. 2007. "Public Transport Subsidies and Affordability in Mumbai, India." Policy Research Working Paper 4395, World Bank, Washington, DC.

Da Mata, Daniel, Uwe Deichmann, J. Vernon Henderson, Somik Lall, and H. G. Wang. 2007. "Determinant of City Growth in Brazil." *Journal of Urban Economics* 62: 252–72.

Dorosh, Paul, and Emily M. Schmidt. 2008. "Mozambique Corridors: Implications of Investments in Feeder Roads." World Bank, Spatial and Local Development Team, Washington, DC.

Economides, Nicholas. 1996. "The Economics of Networks." *International Journal of Industrial Organization* 14 (6): 673–99

Egis Bceom International. 2007. "Study of the Feasibility of Logistics Platforms at Bogotá and the Region of the Savannah of Bogotá." Guyancourt, France.

ESCAP (United Nations Economic and Social Commission for Asia and the Pacific). 2007. "Sustainable Infrastructure in Asia: Overview and Proceedings." Seoul Initiative Policy Forum on Sustainable Infrastructure, Seoul, September 6–8, 2006.

Gómez-Ibáñez, Jose A. 2011. "Urban Transportation and Green Growth." Harvard University, Cambridge, MA.

Gwilliam Ken. 1987. "Market Failures, Subsidy and Welfare Maximisation." In *Transport Subsidy*, ed. Stephen Glaister. Newbury, U.K.: Policy Journals.

———. 2011. *Africa's Transport Infrastructure: Mainstreaming Maintenance and Management*. Washington DC: World Bank.

Henderson, J. Vernon, and Jacques François Thisse, eds. 2004. *Handbook of Regional and Urban Economics*, vol. 4. Amsterdam: Elsevier.

Hidalgo, Dario, Paulo Custodio, and Pierre Graftieaux. 2007. "A Critical Look at Major Bus Improvements in Latin America and Asia:

Case Studies of Hitches, Hic-Ups and Areas for Improvement; Synthesis of Lessons Learned." Summary presentation, World Bank, Washington, DC, April 4.

ITDP (Institute for Transportation and Development Policy). 2007. *Bus Rapid Transit Planning Guide*. New York: ITDP. http://www.itdp.org/microsites/bus-rapid-transit-planning-guide/

Klein, Michael. 2012. "Infrastructure Policy: Basic Design Options." Background paper for this report.

Kopits, Elizabeth, and Maureen Cropper. 2003. "Traffic Fatalities and Economic Growth." Policy Research Working Paper 3035, World Bank, Washington, DC.

Kumar, Ajay, and Fanny Barrett. 2008. *Stuck in Traffic: Urban Transport in Africa*. Washington, DC: World Bank.

Laffont, Jean-Jacques. 1994. "The New Economics of Regulation Ten Years After." *Econometrica* 62 (3): 507–37.

Lall, Somik V., Zmarak Shalizi, and Uwe Deichmann. 2004. "Agglomeration Economies and Productivity in Indian Industry." *Journal of Development Economics* 73 (2): 643–73.

Lall, Somik V., Hyoung Gun Wang, and Thomas Munthali. 2009. "Explaining High Transport Costs within Malawi—Bad Roads or Lack of Trucking Competition?" Policy Research Working Paper 5133, World Bank, Washington, DC.

Lee, Myung-Kyoon. 2003. "TransMilenio Bus Rapid Transit System of Bogota, Colombia." UNEP Collaborating Centre on Energy and Environment, Roskilde, Denmark.

Litman, Todd. 2006. "London Congestion Pricing." Victoria Transport Policy Institute, Victoria, Canada.

McKinsey & Company. 2010. *Building India: Transforming the Nation's Logistics Infrastructure*. Washington, DC.

Menon, A. P. Gopinath. 2002. "Travel Demand Management in Singapore—Why Did It Work?" MSI Global Pte Ltd, Singapore.

Mokhtarian, Patricia L., Michael N. Bagley, and Ilan Salomon. 1998 "The Impact of Gender, Occupation, and Presence of Children on Telecommuting Motivations and Constraints." *Journal of American Society for Information Science* 49 (12): 1115–34.

NEA Transport Research and Training. 2003. "Final Report: Integration and Regulatory

Structures in Public Transport." European Commission GD TREN, Rijswijk, Netherlands.

Newman, Peter, and Jeffrey R. Kenworthy. 1989. *Cities and Automobile Dependence: An International Sourcebook*. Aldershot, U.K.: Avebury.

Samad, Taimur, Nancy Lozano-Gracia, and Alexandra Panman, eds. 2012. *Colombia Urbanization Review: Amplifying the Gains from the Urban Transition*. Directions in Development series. Washington, DC: World Bank.

Schrank, David, Tim Lomax, and Bill Eisele. 2011. "2011 Urban Mobility Report." Texas A&M University, Texas Transportation Institute, College Station, TX.

Stigler, George J. 1971. "The Theory of Economic Regulation." *The Bell Journal of Economics and Management Science* 2 (1): 3–21.

Tao, Zhining, Geoffrey J. D. Hewings, and Kieran P. Donaghy. 2010. "An Economic Analysis of Trends of Mid-Western US Pollutant Emissions from 1970 to 2000." *Ecological Economics* 69 (8): 1666–74.

Teravaninthorn, Supee, and Gaël Raballand. 2009. *Transport Prices and Costs in Africa: A Review of the Main International Corridors*. Washington, DC: World Bank.

Timilsina, Govinda R., and Hari B. Dulal. 2010. "Urban Road Transportation Externalities: Costs and Choice of Policy Instruments." *World Bank Research Observer* 26 (1): 162–91.

Uganda Bureau of Statistics. 2010. Uganda National Household Survey 2009/2010. Kampala.

World Bank. 2004. *Sri Lanka Development Policy Review*. Report No. 29396-LK. Washington, DC: South Asia Region, Poverty Reduction and Economic Management Sector Unit, World Bank.

———. 2006. *Brazil—Inputs for a Strategy for Cities: A Contribution with a Focus on Cities and Municipalities*. Report No. 35749-BR. Washington, DC: Latin America and the Caribbean Region, Finance, Private Sector and Infrastructure Management Unit, World Bank.

———. 2008. *World Development Report 2009: Reshaping Economic Geography*. Washington, DC: World Bank.

———. 2010. *Sri Lanka: Reshaping Economic Geography. Connecting People to Prosperity*. Washington, DC: World Bank.

———. 2011a. "Urbanization Review—Brazil." Washington, DC: Finance, Economics, and Urban Department, Urban and Local Governments Unit, World Bank.

———. 2011b. "Urbanization Review—South Korea." Washington, DC: Korea Research Institute for Human Settlements.

———. 2011c. "Vietnam Urbanization Review." Technical Assistance Report. The World Bank. Washington, D.C.

———. 2012a. *Inclusive Green Growth: The Pathway to Sustainable Development*. Washington, DC: World Bank.

———. 2012b. Planning for Uganda's Urbanization. Inclusive Growth Policy Note 4. World Bank, Washington, DC.

New cities should be well located, flexibly regulated, and efficiently connected: Lessons from China, the Arab Republic of Egypt, and the Republic of Korea on placement, policy, and provision of infrastructure

Cities in the developing world increasingly must accommodate urban ex-pansion. During rapid urbanization, existing cities struggle to cope with infrastructure backlogs and increased densities. Policy makers have two main options: they can expand existing cities—increasing urban areas and densities—or they can create new ones.

New cities have been planned, with mixed success, in countries including China, the Arab Republic of Egypt, and the Republic of Korea. A look at their history suggests two main lessons:

- New cities are more economically viable if they are located near existing metropolitan areas.
- Given a good location, a new city can yield higher returns if it benefits from coordinated policies for land use and for infrastructure—with fluid land markets and strong connections to existing cities.

These two principles—a good location, institutionally supported land use transformation coordinated with connective infrastructure—do much to explain the early success of China's *Jing Ji Te Qu* or special economic zones (SEZs).[1] The Shenzhen SEZ was deliberately located just north of Hong Kong SAR, China, on a greenfield site in southern China. Although basically rural, the area had two urban settlements. One was Luohu, the main customs checkpoint with Hong Kong SAR, China and a major point of cross-border traffic on the Kowloon-Canton Railway. The other was Shenzhen Old Town, a stopover for cross-border travelers (Wong and Yeh 1985).

China's government enabled land use transformation in the Shenzhen SEZ by assembling large lots of land and by adjusting land prices to attract industry. The introduction of land auctions in 1987 led to a boom in property development, while giving the local government more extrabudgetary capital to improve basic and connective infrastructure—ports and roads, water and sewerage, electricity and gas, telephone communications—and to carry out development plans (Zeng 2011). Shenzhen's success revolves around its spatial proximity to Hong Kong SAR, China, but this advantage was supported by strong state actions to nurture land and labor markets. China's government invested in the initial basic and connective infrastructure for SEZs, even as it offered private investors the opportunity to collaborate in infrastructure development. The government also helped entrepreneurs take risks and experiment with new products, in part through subsidized financing (Zeng 2011). And the SEZ was granted considerable autonomy in deciding how to attract industry, including legislative authority: it could develop municipal laws and regulations along the basic lines of national laws and regulations (Zheng 2009). Finally, labor markets were created. Shenzhen was the first zone in China to adopt wage reforms, including a minimum wage and a social insurance package (Sklair 1991).

What happens to new cities planned without regard for the principles of convenient location, flexible regulations, and efficient connections? They fail. Egypt planned and developed 20 towns over the past 20 years to reduce population growth in Cairo and the Nile valley. Meant for 5 million people, the new towns have barely drawn 800,000. In the Greater Cairo Area, eight new towns were created to deconcentrate the city—but by 2006 they still accounted for less than 14 percent of Greater Cairo's population increase over a decade (World Bank 2008a). The reason for these failures is that Egypt's new towns are hobbled by their distant locations, overly rigid land use plans, and lack of connective infrastructure. Their planning norms, considered restrictive by international standards, have elevated property prices and limited affordable housing. And the need for infrastructure to connect the new towns with existing metropolitan markets has been neglected, deterring firms from relocating. Finally, taxes on new trucks are high in Egypt, and important roads are of low quality, so road transport costs are prohibitive (Nathan Associates 1999).

In contrast to Egypt's failed towns, Korea's new cities were a success. Developed mostly over a single five-year period in the mid-1990s, they quickly attracted 2.7 million new residents (Lee and Ahn 2005). During their rise, Seoul was spatially deconcentrated, and its population began a gradual decline. How did Korea ensure that its new cities would be

viable? By basing its regional development plans on the principles of convenient location, flexible regulation, and efficient connection. During the 1980s, as the demand for urban land increased, the government assembled land in Seoul's periphery for five new cities strategically positioned within 20–25 kilometers of the city's central business district (Kim 1999; Korea Land Company n.d.). The land, acquired through public purchase, was fully paid for at market prices. Densification was encouraged by fluid urban development guidelines on issues such as floor area ratio and land conversion. And the new cities were connected to Seoul's core with metro links and with bridges across the Han River (World Bank 2008b).

Rigid policies on land use and urban expansion, with underinvestment in urban infrastructure, will limit the growth of new cities and existing metropolitan areas alike. New cities are likely to do well near existing metropolitan areas, but underlying land market distortions must also be corrected and rights-of-way set aside for infrastructure in greenfield locations (just as infrastructure must be developed in areas already showing economic promise). The suburbs of large metropolitan areas are well suited to the creation of thriving new cities. Developing new cities far from large metropolitan areas is more risky—so before a government plans to develop such locations, it should first carefully assess why they have not already taken off. Is it because of regulatory constraints, high transport costs, or low market accessibility (limiting yields on private investment)? If public investments are made to offset some of these costs, will they succeed in countering the tendency of firms to cluster in sectors that value agglomeration economies? Finally, since agglomeration economics asserts that some metropolitan concentration of economic activity is best for productivity, what is the tradeoff in industrial location between national efficiency and spatial equity?

Around the world, new cities have been seen as solutions to metropolitan problems. But city leaders could more prudently address the problems by encouraging fluid urban land

and labor markets—regardless of whether the solutions include new cities or redeveloping old ones. The main question is not whether the government should or should not initiate the development of new cities. It is whether the government has taken the needed measures to correct underlying land market failures and has created institutions to set aside rights-of-way for infrastructure expansion. With these policies in place, a city can develop organically. In their absence, urban development will falter.

Note

1. Given the strong hand of the government in SEZ development, it may be difficult to replicate China's experience in every detail. But the underlying principles still apply.

References

Kim, Jeong-Ho. 1999. "Public Policies for New Towns in Korea: An Appraisal." Korea Research Institute for Human Settlements, Gyeonggi-do, Korea.

Korea Land Company. n.d. "Overall Assessment of New Towns in the Seoul Metropolitan Area." Seongnam, Korea.

Lee, Chang-Moo, and Kun-Hyuck Ahn. 2005. "Five New Towns in the Seoul Metropolitan Area and Their Attractions in Non-working Trips: Implications on Self-containment of New Towns." *Habitat International* 29: 647–66.

Nathan Associates. 1999. "Reducing Transport Costs of Egypt's Exports." U.S. Agency for International Development, Cairo.

Sklair, Leslie. 1991. "Problems of Socialist Development—the Significance of Shenzhen Special Economic Zone for China Open-Door Development Strategy." *International Journal of Urban and Regional Research* 15 (2): 197–215.

Wong, Aline K., and Stephen Yeh. 1985. *Housing a Nation: 25 Years of Public Housing in Singapore*. Singapore: Maruzen Asia.

World Bank. 2008a. "The Dynamics of Periurban Areas around Greater Cairo Region." Urban Sector Update, Urban Note, March 2008, Cairo.

———. 2008b. *World Development Report 2009: Reshaping Economic Geography*. Washington, DC: World Bank.

Zeng, Douglas Z. 2011. "How Do Special Economic Zones and Industrial Clusters Drive China's Rapid Development?" Policy Research Working Paper 5583, World Bank, Washington, DC.

Zheng, Yu. 2009. "Incentives and Commitment: The Political Economy of Special Zones in China." University of Connecticut, Storrs, CT.

Financing cities

3

Having identified priorities for investments, city leaders confront the problem of financing those investments. The main difficulty is the need for money up front. Large capital outlays are needed to provide infrastructure and services that are not fully in demand now, but will become so as urbanization picks up speed (Mohan 2009). The large capital investments that are needed in the construction phase—whether for transport, water provision, solid waste management, or sewage removal and treatment—are likely to far exceed the budget of any city government (figure 3.1).

How do city leaders bridge the gap between readily available resources and investment needs? What sources should they tap? To start with, the government can establish its creditworthiness by first securing cash flows from user fees and taxes—and by leveraging the value of land in various ways, including taxes. Only with future cash flows secured can the government begin to borrow money and attract private investment.

Whether financing is public or private generally does not make the difference between successful and struggling cities. But there are at least two situations in which private financing may be the preferred course: when

the government sees public-private partnerships (PPPs) as a way toward greater long-term efficiency in service provision, and when the government suffers from severe credit constraints that prevent it from obtaining credit for improvements to a publicly run system.

Infrastructure service providers, whether public or private, will usually benefit from clear government policies that ensure cost recovery through competitive pricing. The value of covering costs through user fees has been emphasized throughout this report.[1] If costs can be covered through prices, then whether ownership is public or private need not make a large difference to city leaders—or to the urban residents who are best served when provision is reliable, affordable, and efficient.

Thus, the primary question for city leaders is not likely to be the question of ownership. (To be sure, policy debates have too often focused on this question—and on details of financial engineering that similarly do not deserve first consideration.) Instead, policy makers are wise to think first about how to secure cash flows for service provision, how to finance improvements by turning a city's existing assets into new ones, and how to

FIGURE 3.1   Mismatch between capital needs and budget resources of city governments

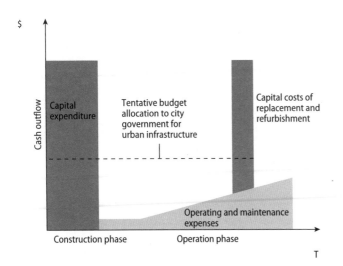

Source: Recreated from KPMG 2010.

create an inviting economic environment for private firms.

To finance investments in infrastructure, city leaders have three main tasks (CDIA 2010; World Bank Institute and PPIAF 2012). They need to:

- *Value and develop the city's creditworthiness.* Creditworthiness can be demonstrated by securing cash flows through user fees and taxes—and, where necessary, by raising revenue through leveraged assets. It is also possible to tap capital markets, either by issuing bonds or by borrowing from specialized financial institutions and intermediaries.
- *Coordinate public and private finance using clear and consistent rules.* With enough assurance that commitments are firm, PPPs can reduce the fiscal burden of infrastructure improvement projects.
- *Leverage existing assets to develop new ones, linking both to land use planning.* Leveraging can include land and property taxes; land sales and leases; charges for impact and for development (developer extractions); betterment levies (land

value capture taxes); and tax increment financing.

The rest of this chapter presents key considerations for city leaders, as they scrutinize these choices and seek the best way to finance their cities' infrastructure needs. Land-based financing instruments and PPPs have both advantages and disadvantages. Neither can turn a project based on bad economics into a good project. Nor is either likely to impose excessive costs. Any decision by city leaders to pursue one financing option rather than another should be made for the sake of efficiency, not finance—except perhaps in times of fiscal crisis, when severe credit constraints may compel government to tap land-based instruments and private finance for additional resources.

Value and develop the city's creditworthiness

City leaders can also consider borrowing to finance infrastructure investments—but borrowing might not be easy. Municipal governments in most developing countries have little access to credit markets, partly because there are no local government credit markets.

Despite this lack of local credit in developing countries, experience in developed countries suggests that local credit can work for long-term municipal financing—if regulations are in place to guide the issuance of debt and manage the risks. Such regulations should clearly set forth procedures for subnational governments to follow when lending money, including the purposes, types, and amounts of allowable loans. They also should clearly define institutional mechanisms for approving loans and monitoring debt (Liu 2010).

Only a strong regulatory framework can enable cities to manage debt and reduce the risk of insolvency. The 1990s saw a widespread subnational debt crisis affecting many countries: Argentina, Brazil, Colombia, Hungary, Mexico, the Russian Federation, South Africa, and others. What those countries needed, but lacked, was a regulatory framework to strengthen subnational fiscal discipline (Liu and Waibel 2008).

Valuing creditworthiness

Even where subnational credit markets exist, it is hard to find useful and reliable information on the creditworthiness of local governments in developing countries—one reason being a lack of transparency in municipal government operations (Kaganova 2011). Developed countries make information on creditworthiness available in the form of bond ratings.

Colombia has promoted transparency by publishing traffic-light ratings of local payment capacity, with red, green, and yellow signals reflecting a combination of liquidity and solvency indicators. To rate municipalities' subnational debt, a red light identifies those whose ratio of interest to operational savings exceeds 40 percent and whose ratio of debt stock to current revenues exceeds 80 percent. Red-light municipalities cannot borrow. Green-light municipalities can. Yellow-light municipalities can borrow only after obtaining the approval of the central government (Liu and Waibel 2008).

In 2010, the Municipality of Lima, Peru, obtained a loan to finance urban infrastructure. As a first step, the city received donor-supported technical assistance to apply for a credit rating from an international rating agency. The outcome was a $70 million commercial bank loan from BBVA Banco Continental to the municipality. This loan took Lima a large step forward to securing long-term financing—its maturity was double that of the city's previous debts, making debt service payments more affordable and freeing municipal revenues to cover critical operating expenses. The loan was partially backed by a $32 million guarantee from the International Finance Corporation (Samad, Lozano-Gracia, and Panman 2012; IFC 2012).

An example involving the water sector is found in Kenya. The Water and Sanitation Program, together with the Water Services Regulatory Board in Kenya, recently completed an effort to establish utility shadow

credit ratings for 43 urban water supply providers. In the process, they found that 13 would be likely to be rated A or BBB creditworthy and 16 BB; these high credits scores may open the door for private commercial finance on the local bond market for these local water suppliers.

Giving smaller cities access to capital markets: bond banks and resource pools

Smaller cities may be unable to gain direct access to long-term credit because they lack the required financial infrastructure and local capacity. In such cases, city leaders can instead seek short- or medium-term loans from higher levels of government through specialized donor-funded entities, such as municipal development funds. Or financial institutions can pool capacities to set up municipal local government financial intermediaries, or bond banks (Samad, Lozano-Gracia, and Panman 2012).

Developed countries with bond banks include Belgium, Finland, France, Spain, and Sweden, as well as Canada with its municipal finance corporations (mostly provincial agencies operating at the provincial level) and the United States with its municipal bond banks (state instrumentalities operating at the state level). Funds may not be available for all projects through bond banks, but they are an important source of funding for cities (Kaganova 2011).

In Colombia, a successful bond bank is FINDETER (Financiera de Desarrollo Territorial), a government company created to finance regional urban infrastructure projects. More than 90 percent nationally owned, with the remainder owned by the *Departamentos*, FINDETER provides resources to financial intermediaries who assign them to regional authorities. It has received funds from multilateral banks and has consistently received very high credit ratings (see spotlight D) (Samad, Lozano-Gracia, and Panman 2012).

Another way to give smaller cities access to capital markets is through resource pools. India has pooled smaller municipalities' resources for this purpose. The first step was to rate municipal credit using a national methodology. In 1995, this methodology was applied to the Ahmedabad Municipal Corporation by Credit Rating Information Services of India Limited. And in 1996, Ahmedabad received a rating for bond offering. In 1998, Ahmedabad issued India's first municipal bond without a state guarantee—a Rs 1 billion bond to finance a water supply and sewerage project. Used in combination with fiscal and management reforms (to computerize accounting, improve tax collection, and the like), the bond issue helped Ahmedabad turn a fiscal deficit into a surplus.

In 2001, the government of India announced guidelines for tax-free municipal bonds. Its aim was to create incentives for local governments to improve their fiscal management and meet the demands of capital markets. Again, Ahmedabad was first to issue the bonds: in 2002, it borrowed Rs 1 billion through a 10-year tax-free bond with 9 percent annual interest.

Because only larger municipalities such as Ahmedabad were able to obtain the credit ratings needed for municipal bond issues, the government of India took a further step: it created special mechanisms to help smaller municipalities pool their resources and jointly access credit. The government's Pooled Finance Development Fund Guidelines are meant to encourage small municipalities in undertaking the fiscal, financial, and institutional reforms that will give them access to market funds (Vaidya and Vaidya 2008; World Bank 2011a).

Another example in India is the Tamil Nadu Urban Development Fund, which converted from a state-owned municipal development fund into India's first financial intermediary, with private sector capital and management participation. It has successfully mobilized financial resources from the capital market, through various innovative financing schemes and helped small municipalities develop PPP projects such as the Build, Operate, and Transfer (BOT) project—for example, the Karur Bridge BOT and Alandur wastewater BOT (see spotlight D).

Is resource pooling the best way for smaller cities to obtain credit? The jury is still out. Pooling can be difficult, as a highly rated government may be reluctant to lend weaker governments the benefit of its credit rating. In such cases, a more realistic alternative is parallel financing: each municipality borrows on its own terms—based on its creditworthiness and ability to pay—to finance a common project (Isabel Chatterton, personal communications, May 2012).

Bond banks and resource pooling—with guarantees—can be used to reduce the risk of smaller government debt. Yet neither is a substitute for establishing the foundations of creditworthiness in local governments (box 3.1). City leaders can help cities establish their creditworthiness by (Pethe and Ghodke 2005):

- Creating credible accounting mechanisms.
- Creating sound financial management systems.
- Requiring the independent auditing of local government finances.
- Requiring performance evaluations for local government services.

Finally, it should be recalled that capital markets—in assessing the risks of municipal government debt—will strongly prefer investment projects designed to cover costs through pricing mechanisms (World Bank Institute and PPIAF 2012).

Besides bond banks and resource pools, another option for accessing credit is private financing through PPPs. Such partnerships are likely to favor cost recovery through user fees in service provision. And they can work well—if they follow rules that are clearly established in advance.

Coordinate public and private finance using clear and consistent rules

Traditionally, urban infrastructure financing has come from higher government levels—which raise the funds through taxes—and from government-owned or government-

BOX 3.1   Subnational debt finance: Making it sustainable

State and local government debt, and debt of quasi-public agencies have been growing in importance. Rapid urbanization, with unprecedented rural-to-urban migration, will continue to demand massive urban infrastructure investments—investments that largely have been decentralized to subnational governments in many countries. Developing countries invest an annual average of 3–4 percent of GDP in infrastructure, well short of what is considered to be required (7–8 percent). The scale and the sustainability of infrastructure financing will critically depend on the subnational government's fiscal sustainability.

The sovereign's macroeconomic fundamentals will continue to be vital to the fiscal sustainability of subnational governments. Major international rating agencies generally cap subsovereign credit ratings by the sovereign credit ratings. A country's macroeconomic management and countrywide risks affect not only the broader economic, fiscal, and financial conditions under which a subnational government operates, but they also place restrictions on its ability to raise funds.

Subnational debt sustainability will also require strong regulatory frameworks for borrowing, including the management of implicit and contingent liabilities. Significant progress has been made in establishing ex ante fiscal rules for subnationals in various developing countries to reduce default risks. Newly decentralizing countries will need to develop regulatory frameworks for subnational debt instruments before opening up subnational government access to financial markets. More also needs to be done in developing a robust ex post insolvency system for debt restructuring in the case of subnational defaults. A sound insolvency system reduces the moral hazard of free-riding on common resources by individual subnationals and sends signals to financial markets about pricing risks and returns.

Many subnational governments have created special-purpose vehicles to undertake infrastructure investments, often in partnership with private financiers and operators. Such vehicles can play an impor-

tant role in developing infrastructure networks that cut across the boundaries of subnational administrations. But the special-purpose vehicle operations must be within a transparent governance and financial structure to ensure that they do not become a means of circumventing borrowing limits or contingent liabilities of their creators.

Land asset–based financing is an additional and important source of subnational finance for urban infrastructure in many countries, as land is often the most valuable asset on the asset side of subnational balance sheets. It can also create significant fiscal risks, including diverting proceeds for current expenditure and using land and other hard assets as collateral for debt instruments such as bank loans. The upswing in the value of hard assets in economic booms can lead to excessive borrowing; and the volatility of land and real estate markets creates risks for nonperforming loans, which can create macroeconomic risks.

The global financial crisis has brought home the importance of developing domestic financial markets, including subnational credit markets. Subnational governments or their entities in various countries have already issued bond instruments (for example, in China, Colombia, India, Mexico, Poland, the Russian Federation, and South Africa). More countries are considering policy frameworks for facilitating subnational debt market development (Indonesia), whereas others are allowing selected subnational entities to pilot-test transaction and capacity-building activities (Peru). A competitive and diversified subnational credit market can help ensure the lowest cost and the sustainable availability of credit. This means opening access on equal terms to bank lending and bond issuance and prohibiting monopolies of "municipal or development banks." Securities laws and market infrastructure are part of developing subnational credit markets.

Contributed by Lili Liu, based on Canuto and Liu (2010), Liu (2010), Liu and Pradelli (2012), and Liu and Tan (2009).

sponsored banks and financial institutions. But because the political costs for these expenditures have been borne at the national level, towns and cities have not always had strong

incentives to manage risks wisely, to spend money efficiently, or to do what is needed for continued creditworthiness. Cities are more accountable for their own development when

---

BOX 3.2   Paying for infrastructure through ancillary services

When infrastructure services cannot easily cover their full cost through user fees, ancillary services can sometimes fill the gap.

For example, a toll road operator may not be able to set fees high enough to cover costs. But there is money to be made in roadside businesses. So city leaders can combine the toll road franchise with the right to lease out service concessions for hotels, restaurants, or gas stations at highway rest stops. Indeed, a toll road company might lease out the rights to real estate development along part, or all, of a highway.

In granting a highway concession, governments can thus auction off the full package of rights and obligations to obtain the best price for the whole. Similarly, one of the main revenue sources for an airport franchise is the right to operate or lease out concession services—shops, restaurants, and the like—at the airport. Such add-ons to basic infrastructure service can make funding possible without recourse to regular government budgets. And when infrastructure service is independent of fiscal processes, the government is better insulated from undue political influence.

Still, there is a danger that subsidies may become excessive and foster economically inefficient projects. So city leaders should routinely use cost-benefit analyses to measure the welfare increases that infrastructure services are likely to produce.

Sources: Klein 2012.

---

the funds for that development are raised locally.

One way for cities to raise funds locally and demonstrate accountability is through PPPs. City leaders in developing countries—where financial markets do not readily allow municipalities to access long-term credit—are especially likely to think about private participation in urban infrastructure projects.

Done well, PPPs can not only attract additional infrastructure financing but also improve project selection—ensuring that selected projects are sustainable by subjecting them to private sector market selection mechanisms. In addition, PPPs can improve asset utilization and favor cost recovery through user fees. User fees are not exclusive to PPPs, since governments also can charge users to cover costs. Yet governments may find it politically difficult to achieve full cost recovery through user fees. Using ancillary benefits to recover costs may also be a politically viable alternative (box 3.2).

In addition, it may be difficult or impossible for the government—even after announcing that it will cover costs through a regime of user fees—to obtain financing for improvements in public infrastructure service provision. When services are to be publicly provided (or provided through state-owned enterprises), lenders do not always accept a government's assurances about cost recovery through user fees. Why? One reason is that lenders lack confidence in the government's commitment to fee collection (fees actually collected might differ from those initially announced). Another is that lenders fear a diversion of fee revenues from cost recovery—their original purpose—to other uses. Uncertainty of demand may also be a concern. Finally, lenders can be wary of unpredictable leadership, wondering whether a state-owned service provider will have its revenues arbitrarily taxed or withheld by the government.

When lenders remain reluctant to extend credit even after user fees are announced, the government may have no choice. The only way for city leaders to restore credit and finance urban infrastructure projects may then be through the sale of public assets to private firms.[2]

Private participation is not a magic bullet against all challenges to infrastructure financing. Further, the contractual arrangements for PPPs can vary considerably depending on the risk allocated to the private sector (table 3.1). Like any other financing source, PPPs require commitments from sustainable cost-covering tariffs or equivalent tax revenues. Because long-term fiscal commitments depend on risky variables—such as costs, demand, or exchange rates—their cost can be difficult to assess. They may prompt over-commitment from the government and excessive fiscal risk, because the cost of guarantees offered may be hard to estimate (World Bank Institute and PPIAF 2012).

In 1990, the government of Colombia provided guarantees on toll road revenues, airport revenues, and payments to utility (power) companies under long-term purchase agreements. The government underestimated the risks of these guarantees—among other problems, demand was lower than expected. By 2005, the government had paid out $2 million on the guarantees. Another example of underestimated risks is Korea. In 1990, Korea's government guaranteed 90 percent of forecast revenue for 20 years on a privately financed road linking Seoul to a new airport at Incheon. Again, the government paid tens of millions of dollars every year because demand was lower than expected (World Bank Institute and PPIAF 2012).

In Bolivia, the government privatized the water supply system in the city of Cocha-bamba, awarding a 40-year concession to the private consortium, *Aguas del Tunari*. The contract was awarded without adequate appraisal of the financial situation of the company. Once the concession was awarded, rate structures were modified resulting in increases of up to $20 in water bills, representing as much as 20 percent of incomes for local families. Subsequent violent protests led to *Aguas del Tunari* withdrawing from the project. And in Poland, the government awarded a concession to the Gdansk Transport Company in 1997 for building and operating a section of the highway between Gdansk and Torun. However, a key piece of PPP legislation was missing, delaying the signing of the contract by seven years (World Bank Institute and PPIAF 2012).

TABLE 3.1   Basic options for public-private partnerships

Allocation of risk to private sector	Type of ownership arrangement
None	State-owned enterprise
Service delivery for state-owned firm	Service contract
Management service for a franchise	Management contract
Commercial operations of a franchise (including risk of nonpayment)	Lease, *affermage*
Commercial operations and investment	Concession, privatization

Source: Klein 2012.
Note: There is no significant difference between a full concession and privatization of a monopoly franchise. Compare the French water concessions with English water privatization. An English private owner cannot decide to turn off taps nor can she dig up the pipelines and take them elsewhere. Both concessions and privatizations can be terminated for fault or even without fault. While the details of these two types of contracts may vary, the basics are no different.

In short, PPPs are not a substitute for good financial management and good project evaluation. Examples around the world suggest that when the risks are underestimated, feasibility studies overlooked, and financial sustainability ignored, failure is the result. Policy makers can benefit from PPPs, while avoiding their pitfalls, by following proven rules (box 3.3).

In South Africa, which has a long history of successful infrastructure financing through PPPs, the law that governs them was enacted in 1999. The regulation defines the process for creating a PPP, with the necessary requirements and approvals, and it spells out the institutional responsibilities of all entities involved. Each step in the process is clearly defined in an independent module, which can be updated separately as conditions change—making the regulation flexible and adaptable. The treasury conducts approvals and reviews, evaluating projects with a focus on their affordability and value for money. And the auditor general oversees the entire process, auditing contracting authorities annually to ensure that they follow the rules for PPP implementation.

In many jurisdictions, finally, a clear definition of property rights can provide stronger protection for investors than any promises by the state or its enterprises can. This form of collateralization can make finance flow to infrastructure ventures and help expand systems.

BOX 3.3   Implementing public-private partnerships—lessons from Chile and Mexico

Experience worldwide suggests that successful implementation of public-private partnerships (PPPs) hinges on several key rules. Among these is the need for strong public sector capacity, appropriate legal and sector framework, rigorous planning and risk assessment through feasibility studies, transparent and competitive procurement, strong monitoring systems, and flexibility for adapting to unpredictable events.

Chile's road concession PPPs reflected these rules. Between 1993 and 2001, the government of Chile awarded contracts for 21 roads on a competitive basis. The bidding started with smaller projects in order to test the market while also minimizing the risk for the private sector. More than 40 Chilean and international companies from 10 countries participated in the bidding through 27 consortia. A clear and transparent procurement process, a focus on

public awareness of the process, and a learning-by-doing approach that allowed for adjustments during the process contributed to the success of these PPPs.

In contrast, Mexico's road concessions were not as successful. Between 1987 and 1995, 52 PPPs for toll roads were awarded by the government of Mexico. Average actual revenues for most projects were about 30 percent below forecasts while construction cost overruns averaged 25 percent. A short concession period (with a 15-year maximum) led to high tolls, which increased on average by $0.15 per kilometer after the concessions were granted. This led to the government finally taking over 23 projects and paying outstanding debt to Mexican banks and construction companies, representing about $7.6 billion.

Source: Hodge 2006.

Leverage existing assets to develop new assets

Cities can leverage the value of their assets—mainly land—to finance public infrastructure. An advantage of land-based financing over other sources is that it usually generates more cash up front (CDIA 2010).

Auction mechanisms are often used to sell land in developing countries, which lack systematic land valuations. Some countries use land parcel auctions as a standard element in land management. Land auction data are not widely available—but three recent large transactions illustrate the revenue potential of land auctions (Peterson 2007; Peterson and Kaganova 2010):

- In Cairo, in 2007, the auction of 3,100 hectares of desert land for a new town generated $3.12 billion—an amount 117 times greater than the country's total urban property tax collections, and about a tenth the size of national government revenue. The proceeds were to be used to reimburse costs of internal infrastructure and build a connecting highway to Cairo's ring road.

- In Mumbai, in 2006–07, the auction of 13 hectares of land in the new financial center—Bandra-Kurla Complex—generated $1.2 billion. That was more than 10 times the total 2005 fiscal spending of the Mumbai Metropolitan Regional Development Authority, and 6 times the total value of municipal bonds issued by all urban local bodies and local utilities in India in more than a decade.[3] The proceeds were to be used primarily in financing projects identified by the Metropolitan Transportation Plan.

- In Istanbul, in 2007, the auction of an old bus station and government building generated $1.5 billion—more than the city's total 2005 fiscal expenditures and infrastructure investments.[4]

Clearly, land sales can help to finance urban infrastructure and other investments. Yet city leaders should recognize that all successful land-based financing instruments require at least three kinds of rules to be in place (see chapter 1 on planning). First are rules to assign and protect property rights. Second are institutions for the valuation and public dissemination of land values across various uses. Third is a strong legal framework, with a healthy judicial system to handle disputes and oversee the land-based financing process. Furthermore, a single planning strategy should integrate land-based financing with urban land use planning.

Where governments want to continue owning land, leaseholds have emerged as another way of leveraging land's value. They have been used extensively in China, where the government owns all land.[5] Until 1994, the central government was allowed to collect up to 60 percent of all land leasing revenue. After financial reforms, it went down to 5 percent, enabling local governments to capture a local revenue source (Peterson 2007). China acquires leasable land through several sources. Often it moves administrative buildings or state-owned enterprises to new sites—freeing up desirable spots to be leased—or it acquires rural land from collectives on a city's fringes (Peterson 2007). However, relying extensively on land leases as a revenue source risks creating inefficiencies (at least in the short term) by producing empty or underused new cities in the middle of nowhere. The essential principle is to leverage land to generate new assets, at the same time systematically linking this new revenue source to a city's land use plans.

Land sales and leaseholds can generate initial capital to defray the first-time costs of infrastructure investments. But in the long run, other instruments, such as property taxes and similar levies, must pay for the maintenance and expansion of public facilities. In the United States, property taxes are the main source of revenue for local governments. By contrast, in developing countries, such taxes are still only a small percentage of local revenues—except in the largest cities, where they are becoming more important. One problem is that these taxes are often hard to collect in developing countries, where property values are not systematically defined and tax collection rates are low.

Betterment levies, special assessment taxes, and exactions respond to these challenges by linking fee payments to value increases driven by infrastructure improvement. The funds generated are used to finance the infrastructure projects. To be sure, such projects do not pay their own way. Yet they mesh with local revenue generation and accounting efforts.

A more advanced type of land-based financing, seen in the United States, is tax increment financing. It uses property tax increases from improvements to finance infrastructure investments. Like betterment levies, tax increment financing requires a well-established, functioning property tax regime.

Considered as financing sources for infrastructure investment, land sales may appear simpler than levies, taxes, and exactions. Yet for land sales to immediately raise revenue, they also require strong institutions—particularly institutions of two types:

- Institutions that manage land assets using transparent, robust municipal accounting methods.
- Institutions that determine leasing and sales prices (or floor prices in land sale auctions) by defining objective land valuation techniques.

Furthermore, land sales are a one-time income flow—not a long-term flow to meet a city's ongoing need for financing.

Betterment levies in Colombia and Peru

Betterment levies are payments made by *affected* property owners who help fund infrastructure improvements based on the increased value of their property. Special assessment taxes similarly collect payments from property owners within a designated area of improvement. The best-known system of municipal financing through betterment levy collection is Colombia's. Its betterment levies, or *contribución de valorización,* established in 1921, are now regulated under a law passed in 1970. They have substantially helped to finance local projects, comprising 16 percent of Bogotá's total income in the 1960s (rising to 24 percent in 1993) and 45 percent of Medellín's (Uribe

2010; Borrero 2011).[6] In Bogotá, as much as half of the city's arterial road network was funded by betterment levies (Uribe 2010).

However, a recent study has found three internal challenges to Bogotá's betterment levy system (Uribe 2010). They are:

- *Institutional limitations.* At present managed by the Instituto de Desarrollo Urbano (Urban Development Institute, IDU), the levies were marred until recently by inconsistent property value estimates arising from a lack of communication between the IDU and the cadastre office. Now, updates to the cadastral database enable the IDU to use the property values recorded in the cadastre. Efforts are under way to centralize data collection in the cadastre for the benefit of other institutions.
- *Regressive effects.* Most betterment projects are carried out wherever residents can

pay for them—so they end up benefiting the city's more affluent areas.
- *Poor coordination among various administrations.* Although the IDU works with the planning department on betterment projects, the projects are not always consistent with the city's master plan.

Peru's experience with betterment levies offers an instructive contrast with Colombia's. Concentrated in metropolitan Lima, betterment projects in Peru have yet to gain traction. Why? Because Lima presents them with unique challenges. Although Peru's methodology for betterment levies is nearly identical to Colombia's, a lack of training and of technical knowledge for implementation in Lima means that missteps are common. Over 1990–93, of more than 500 public works projects begun in Lima, only 31 used betterment levy financing (Huayapa 2001).

BOX 3.4   Leveraging land to finance infrastructure: Four lessons from international experience

Strong institutions are needed to make land-based financing instruments work. Institutions are essential to clearly define property rights; to objectively value land using standard methods; and to support and oversee land management, land sales, and tax collection.

Land sales are most successful when coupled with other financing sources, such as a system of property taxes. Although useful as an initial source of revenue for infrastructure investments, land sales are not a reliable source of long-term financing; for that, a tax revenue system is needed.

Betterment levies and special assessment taxes bring revenue to municipalities based on the increase in land value from public improvements. The main challenge to betterment levies, in practice, is determining how to calculate the increases in property value due to improvements. Such determinations require institutions for valuation and for the collection and publication of price data. A simplified solution has worked well in Bogotá: levies are not estimated for each parcel but linked to a citywide

fee. The success of this system is attributable partly to major efforts at updating and maintaining a comprehensive cadastral database—but also to growing citizen participation and oversight.

Development and impact fees, and tax increment financing, are seen mostly in developed countries—because their success requires strong institutions that many developing counties do not yet have. These instruments need a strong regulatory authority to enforce fee collection and to ensure that fees are used only for their defined purpose. Clearly defined property rights are essential. Other prerequisites for success include updated information on property values and a clearly defined methodology for estimating a project's impact on land and property values. And for tax increment financing, a well-developed property tax regime is also required. Unless a strong property tax system is in place, imposing development and impact fees and establishing tax increment financing may be unrealistic ambitions.

Source: Urbanization Review Team.

To succeed, betterment levies require the presence of several factors. One is strong institutions—to collect the taxes and to build project capacity. Another is a clear understanding among taxpayers of how the levy's distribution is defined and how its benefits are calculated. Finally, a positive attitude among taxpayers is essential: encouraging citizen participation and working toward a strong tax payment culture are key steps toward the successful use of betterment levies (box 3.4).

Land-based infrastructure financing has the biggest payoff where there is rapid urban growth. Rapid growth causes land prices to rise rapidly, creating an opportunity to generate significant revenue. Yet rapid growth also magnifies infrastructure investment needs, requiring significant sources of development finance. France, Japan, and the United States used land-based financing techniques most heavily during periods of rapid urban growth when there were large leaps in the scale of urban investment.

As city leaders consider financing infrastructure with land-based instruments, they should also appreciate the risks (Peterson 2007). Real estate markets are highly cyclical. So if land financing is used to finance infrastructure broadly (rather than being dedicated to new development), it will add uncertainty to local government budgets. Furthermore, the large revenues associated with land transactions and urban infrastructure investment create incentives for abuse by intermediaries. Finally, there is a risk that high potential profits from land transactions will transform local authorities into real estate developers, seeking their own profit over the citizens' common welfare.

Notes

1. Prices should cover costs wherever possible and should emerge through competition, or by regulations that mimic competition (discussed in chapters 1 and 2).
2. This position is consistent with the strongest evidence on the superiority of private solutions over public ones (Galal and Nauriyal 1995). According to analyses of infrastructure

privatization during its heyday in the 1990s, the main benefit from privatization was the relaxation of constraints on investment—leading to system expansion and greater overall benefits, as well as to the liquidity that can be critical for governments with credit constraints.
3. Of course, comparing a one-time sale of land with annual fiscal spending should not prompt generalizations about the revenue potential of land sales compared with other financing sources. Without time-series data, it is not clear whether such land sales are fiscally sustainable in the long run.
4. This property in Turkey was purchased by Sama Dubai with grand plans to build the Dubai Towers in Istanbul—to be the tallest skyscrapers in Turkey. However, the municipality and developer could not come to terms on the impact of the buildings to the surrounding area so the project has been halted indefinitely. Meanwhile, the land remains undeveloped.
5. The United Kingdom and Commonwealth countries are other examples.
6. Medellín discontinued the use of betterment levies in 2001 because of administrative challenges.

References

Borrero, Oscar. 2011. "Betterment Levy in Colombia: Relevance, Procedures, and Social Acceptability." *Land Lines* April: 14–19. Lincoln Institute of Land Policy, Cambridge, MA.

Canuto, Otaviano, and Lili Liu. 2010. "Subnational Debt Finance: Make it Sustainable." In *The Day After Tomorrow: A Handbook on the Future of Economic Policy in the Developing World*, ed. Otaviano Canuto and Marcelo Giugale, 219–38. Washington, DC: World Bank.

CDIA (Cities Development Initiative for Asia). 2010. "PPP Guide for Municipalities." Metro Manila, Philippines, June. http://cdia.asia/wp-content/uploads/PPP-Guide-for-Municipalities-FINAL-100609.pdf.

Galal, Ahmed, and Bharat Nauriyal. 1995. "Regulation of Telecom in Developing Countries: Outcomes, Incentives and Commitment." *Revista de Análisis Económico* 10: 41–62.

Hodge, Graeme A. 2006. "Public-Private Partnerships and Legitimacy." *University of New South Wales Law Journal* 29 (3): 318–27.

Huayapa, Margarita. 2001. "Experience with the Betterment Levy in Peru." Working Paper, Lincoln Institute of Land Policy, Cambridge, MA.

IFC (International Finance Corporation). 2012. "Cities and PPPs." *Handshake* 4 (January).

Kaganova, Olga. 2011. *Guidebook on Capital Investing Planning for Local Governments.* Washington, DC: World Bank.

Klein, Michael. 2012. "Infrastructure Policy: Basic Design Options." Background paper for this report.

KPMG. 2010. *Linking Cities to Finance: Overcoming Bottlenecks to Financing Strategic Urban Infrastructure Investments.* Background paper, Shanghai, China, September 27–28.

Liu, Lili. 2010. "Strengthening Subnational Debt Financing and Managing Risks." *Review of Economic Research*; Ministry of Finance, Beijing; August 16, 2010, 46 F-9.

Liu, Lili, and Juan Pradelli. 2012. "Financing Infrastructure and Monitoring Fiscal Risks." Policy Research Working Paper 6069, World Bank, Washington, DC.

Liu, Lili, and Kim S. Tan. 2009. "Subnational Credit Ratings: A Comparative Review." Policy Research Working Paper 5013, World Bank, Washington, DC.

Liu, Lili, and Michael Waibel. 2008. "Managing Subnational Credit and Default Risks." Policy Research Working Paper 5362, World Bank, Washington, DC.

Mohan, Rakesh. 2009. "Global Financial Crisis—Causes, Impact, Policy Responses and Lessons." 7th Annual India Business Forum Conference, London Business School, London, April 23.

Peterson, George E. 2007. "Land Leasing and Land Sale as an Infrastructure Financing Option." In *Financing Cities: Fiscal Responsibility and Urban Infrastructure in Brazil, China, India, Poland and South Africa*, ed. George E. Peterson and Patricia Clarke Annez, 284–306. Washington, DC: World Bank.

Peterson, George E., and Olga Kaganova 2010. "Integrating Land Financing into Subnational Fiscal Management." Policy Research Working Paper 5409, World Bank, Washington, DC.

Pethe, Abhay, and Manju Ghodke. 2005. "Towards Bank Financing of Urban Infrastructure." Working Paper 2, University of Mumbai, Department of Economics.

Samad, Taimur, Nancy Lozano-Gracia, and Alexandra Panman. 2012. *Colombia Urbanization Review: Amplifying the Gains from Urban Transition.* Directions in Development Series. Washington, DC: World Bank.

Uribe, Maria C. 2010. "Land Information Updating, a De Facto Tax Reform: Bringing Up to Date the Cadastral Database of Bogota." In *Innovations in Land Rights Recognition, Administration and Governance*, ed. Klaus Deininger, Clarissa Augustinas, Stig Enemark, and Paul Munro-Faure, 180–207. Washington, DC: World Bank.

Vaidya, Chetan, and Hitesh Vaidya. 2008. "Creative Financing of Urban Infrastructure in India through Market-based Financing and Public-Private Partnership Options." Presented at the 9th Metropolitan Congress, Sydney, October 22–26. http://niua.org/present_series/syndey/sydney_paper.pdf.

World Bank. 2011a. "Developing a Regulatory Framework for Municipal Borrowing in India." Washington, DC: World Bank.

World Bank Institute and PPIAF (Public-Private Infrastructure Advisory Facility). 2012. *Public-Private Partnerships Reference Guide. Version 1.0.* Washington, DC: World Bank.

Innovations in municipal finance: FINDETER and TNUDF

Territorial

In Colombia, commercial banks had no experience with lending to municipal governments until the early 1990s. However, the subsovereign debt market has rapidly developed since, and has been stimulated by the financial intermediation of Financiera de Desarrollo Territorial (FINDETER). FINDETER, established in 1999 as a legally independent and quasi-public financial institution, acts as a second-tier lender encouraging commercial lenders (first-tier lenders) to directly finance municipal governments. By lowering the cost of loans, FINDETER increased commercial banks' willingness to lend to municipal governments.

FINDETER rediscounts loans that commercial banks make to subnational borrowers; this process makes it more financially attractive for commercial banks to lend to subnational borrowers. In practice, this means that a municipal government applies for a loan to a commercial bank. The commercial bank and FINDETER then appraise the proposal and, if approved, the commercial bank lends to the municipal government. FINDETER, in turn, lends an agreed-upon amount at a discounted rate to

the commercial bank. The commercial bank remains responsible for servicing its rediscounted loan by FINDETER regardless of its own collection of debt services from the municipal government, thus absorbing all the credit risk. The municipal government also has to set up a special account into which intergovernmental payments flow. The commercial bank has a senior right to intercept revenue if loan payments are due. The commercial bank, in turn, endorses these liens to FINDETER. Thus, if a participating bank becomes insolvent, FINDETER can still collect its dues (figure SD.1).

FINDETER has encouraged commercial banks to offer municipal governments long-term loans at attractive rates. In addition, it provides long-term financing up to 15 years, whereas typical maximum loan maturities are 3–5 years. From 1990 to 2003, FINDETER has financed about $2 billion in loans in more than 700 municipalities, and from 2006 to 2010, it disbursed about $4 billion. In addition, FINDETER has maintained low levels of bad debt to under 2 percent.

FINDETER has succeeded in establishing itself as a viable financial institution. And although FINDETER initially relied

FIGURE SD.1   FINDETER operational process

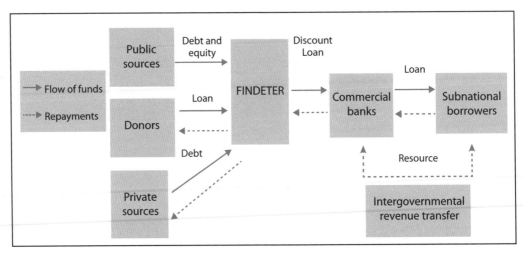

Source: Contributed by Nozomi Tokiwa and Hiroaki Suzuki.

on donor support, primarily from the Inter-American Development Bank and the World Bank, revenue from existing loans has financed more than 78 percent of its activities since 2006. In addition, FINDETER has achieved an AAA local credit rating (from Duff & Phelps), which has helped accessing less expensive financing.

Tamil Nadu Urban Development Fund

In the late 1990s, the government of Tamil Nadu in India faced the challenge of reducing the huge backlog of needed infrastructure investments and of meeting the undersupply of basic urban services. The situation was caused by urban local bodies' limited financial and technical capacity and lack of long-term financing. To solve these problems, the government established the Tamil Nadu Urban Development Fund (TNUDF) in 1996 as the first public-private financial intermediary in India, which aims to provide long-term financing for urban infrastructure in Tamil Nadu. Further, TNUDF's broad scope includes attracting private capital into urban infrastructure and facilitating urban

local bodies' access to capital markets (figure SD.2).

TNUDF has an efficient institutional and managerial framework. They are an autonomous legal entity, outside the government, and also involve equity contributions from three Indian private financial institutions. This structure has facilitated a positive relationship with the private sector, and it has facilitated efficient investment decisions.

TNUDF has mobilized private capital by issuing bonds and by facilitating innovative financing schemes such as credit pooling, securitization, and public-private financing.

- *Bond issuance.* In 2000, TNUDF succeeded in issuing domestic bonds ($59.3 million equivalent) with an LAA rating, indicating high safety and moderate risk due to TNUDF's strong financial position. This was the first nonguaranteed and unsecured bond issuance by a financial intermediary in India.
- *Pool financing.* TNUDF facilitated a credit pooling facility for financing smaller urban local bodies, who face limited financing capacity. In this scheme, small water and sanitation projects were pooled together

FIGURE SD.2   Tamil Nadu Urban Development Fund institutional framework

Source: Contributed by Nozomi Tokiwa and Hiroaki Suzuki.
Note: GTN = government of Tamil Nadu; ULBs = urban local governments; TA = technical assistance.

in a single bond issuance, to be repaid through project revenue. The issuance received a rating of AA by Fitch Ratings.

- *Securitization.* TNUDF structured refinancing of the Madurai Bypass, the first toll road project based on user charge. After the facility began generating revenue, the urban local body issued bonds to refinance the loan made by TNUDF at lower interest rates. The bonds were fully subscribed by banks and other investors.
- *Public-private partnership (PPP) financing:* TNUDF assisted refinancing of Karur Bridge, the first Build, Operate, and Transfer toll bridge in India, through PPP financing. The bond issue was backed by a contract that allows the builder/owner to

increase the toll by 8 percent a year. The project included a substantial equity contribution by the builder/owner.

A high loan recovery rate at around 98 percent has allowed TNUDF to finance and support extended urban infrastructure projects (181 loans to 732 urban local bodies with a cumulative approved loan amount of $95 million as of February 2002). Additionally, the success of TNUDF has been supported from various donors such as the World Bank, the Asian Development Bank, the Japanese International Cooperation Agency, and the KfW banking group in Germany.

Contributed by Nozomi Tokiwa and Hiroaki Suzuki.

4

Framework in action: Lessons from Urbanization Reviews

This chapter presents case studies of seven Urbanization Review pilot countries—Brazil, China, Colombia, India, Indonesia, the Republic of Korea, and Vietnam—with lessons from each.

BRAZIL

Eighty-four percent of Brazil's population lives in urban areas, and urban population growth is expected to drive future population growth. Over 1970–2000, the urban share of Brazil's population climbed from 56 to 82 percent (figure 4.1). Brazil's cities generate about 90 percent of GDP. With this burgeoning urban population, Brazil must successfully manage planning and connecting across the system of cities.

How Brazil is urbanizing

Large urban centers (populations greater than 100,000) dominate Brazil's system of cities. While this system varies considerably by region, 60 percent of all municipalities

The Brazil Urbanization Review has been prepared by a team led by Nancy Lozano-Gracia comprising Hyoung Gun Wang, Henry Jewell, Somik V. Lall, and Eugenia Suarez. Consultants involved in this work were Geoffrey J. D. Hewings, Andre M. Maghalaes, Roberta de Moraes Rocha, and Marcelo E. Alves da Silva.

have populations greater than 100,000 (figure 4.2). These cities are more prevalent in the southeast, where 70 percent of the urban population lives in large urban centers and 23 percent in metropolises (with an urban population of more than 4 million). But Brazil's 12 metropolitan areas have been losing ground as smaller cities attract more people—the percentage of urban population living in the 12 metropolitan areas rose between the 1940s and 1970 but has fallen since.

Home to the vast majority of the country's population, Brazil's cities are the center of economic activity. Today, Brazil mirrors the behavior of developed countries, where income starts to disperse as the country approaches high-income levels. The share in GDP of the 12 largest metropolitan areas has been declining slowly, from about 46 percent in 2000 to about 43 percent in 2008. São Paolo and Rio de Janeiro led the decline, moving from about 33 to 30 percent in these eight years. Dispersion of GDP may also be related to the decline in productivity growth in the past years in larger cities, as well as to increased congestion, bad management,

FIGURE 4.1   Brazil's rapid urbanization: From 30 percent urban in 1940 to 84 percent in 2010

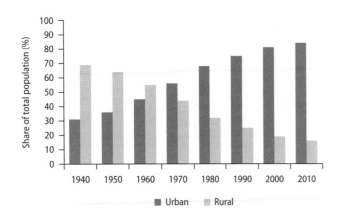

Source: IBGE demographic census, several years.

FIGURE 4.2   More than half of Brazil's urban population (60 percent) is in large cities

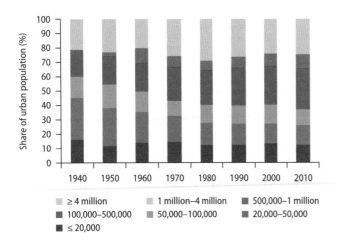

Source: IBGE demographic census, several years.

and poor metropolitan coordination, among other problems (World Bank 2006).

Despite great population inflows into cities, Brazil has been closing the gap in access to basic services across city sizes. In 1990, the gap in access to piped water between small and large cities was about 30 percentage points; by 2000, this gap closed to about 13 percentage points. Access to piped water was already above 85 percent across cities at that time. While for other basic services such as sewerage the gap in access between city sizes is still large (more than 40 percentage points), it declined by 10 percentage points in those 10 years. Considerable regulatory reforms in water and electricity in the second half of the 1990s contributed to this success. And tariffs have helped extend the networks and expand access.

Brazil's system of cities follows the patterns suggested by international experience, indicating that the system is well integrated and that different cities are performing different activities (figure 4.3). As one would expect in an integrated urban system, large cities are diversified and small and medium cities are more specialized. Between 1995 and 2008, the Herfindahl-Hirschman Index[1] for production activity increased in medium cities, small cities, and mostly rural municipalities, suggesting more concentrated production activities.

Location quotients[2] for the 123 largest urban agglomerations confirm the national pattern. The largest cities have a strong concentration of high and medium-high technology industries like publishing; chemical products; and electrical, electronic, and transportation equipment. Computer-related industries and financial services are also clustered in the largest cities. Medium cities host industries of medium technological levels, such as textiles and pulp and paper products. Low technology industries are most commonly in the smallest cities (Da Mata and others 2006; 2007). Different cities in Brazil seem to be performing different functions, as expected in a well-connected system.

Urban challenges

Access to basic services

Regional and within-city disparities in access to basic services persist. While Brazil has improved access to water and electricity, there are still considerable differences in access to basic services across the urban system. The gap in access to piped water is closing. But the north region seems to be lagging. Average access to piped water in medium cities was below 60 percent in 2000. Disparities are also wide within cities: while on average only 8 percent of total households do not have a bathroom within their house, the percentage in slum households is 12 percent.

These regional differences may lead to migrants moving for the wrong reasons. When people migrate in search of better access to basic services, location decisions may lead to inefficient outcomes. These individuals may end up contributing more to congestion in large cities than to increases in agglomeration benefits. A study of Brazilian migration finds that higher wages in leading regions is a strong determinant of the decision to migrate. But it also finds that many individuals migrate in search of better access to basic services (Lall, Timmons, and Yu 2009).

Connective infrastructure and transport costs

Connective infrastructure is deteriorating due to lack of maintenance. Large investments in connective infrastructure in the 1950s and 1970s paid off. But the paved road network has deteriorated, and overall road conditions are similar to those in the 1970s (World Bank 2006). Large portions of federal and state networks have paved roads that are old, without proper maintenance for many years. While less than 30 percent of the roads were considered of bad quality in 2000, by 2007 that percentage rose to more than 40. Less than 35 percent of the roads were considered of good quality in 2007. Transport costs have risen steadily by around 5 percent per year. More important, in the past three years the highest increases appear to be for short-distance trips.

Housing deficits

In both rural and urban areas, housing deficits are large. The urban housing deficit represents between 60 and 90 percent of the total deficit, depending on the region.

FIGURE 4.3 High specialization in smaller municipalities—greater diversity in large cities

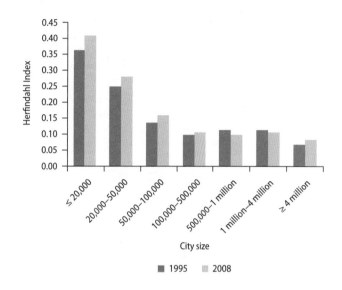

Sources: Employment data at 2–4 digit industrial classification; Relação Anual de Informações Sociais/ Ministerio do Trabalho e Emprego data for 1995 and 2008; authors' calculations.

Housing deficits in urban areas vary between 7 percent in the south and 32 percent in the north. In rural areas, the deficits for these two regions are 9 and 44 percent, respectively. While the housing deficit is larger in relative terms in urban areas, the number of units is much larger given the high urbanization rate of the country.

Urban density

With density increasing in Brazil's largest cities, congestion will worsen, making an efficient transport system even more important. A city that wants to grow denser must recognize that a dense city is feasible only when workers can commute efficiently to their workplaces. Between 2001 and 2009, commutes up to 30 minutes appear to have remained relatively stable or declined in most cities. But a combination of relocation of some major economic activities, changes in residential locations, and increased congestion generated by dramatic growth in car ownership have stretched commuting times in places like São Paulo and Salvador.

Congestion also leads to considerable environmental impacts such as pollution.

High poverty and income disparities

Between 1991 and 2000, the number of people living on less than half minimum wage declined only slightly.[3] The northeast and the north have a considerably larger percentage in poverty than the leading region of southeast. And the pattern across city sizes didn't vary between 1991 and 2000: the largest metropolitan areas have less poverty than smaller cities and mostly rural municipalities. In all regions, the percentage of poor in small and medium cities is growing over time. The total number of poor is also higher in municipalities with smaller urban populations. More important, the number of poor in large cities has remained fairly constant.

Other challenges

Brazil's cities face metropolitan management issues and safety and crime control. Brazil's metropolitan regions and other large agglomerations in many cases still lack metropolitan management, and planning is done at the municipality level.

Looking ahead

Planning

Stringent land regulations led to dramatic growth in slums in the last 60 years, and today about 60 percent of urban land is under some kind of informality (World Bank 2006). The annual growth of slum dwellers in cities in the 1980s and 1990s were 5.5 and 3.9 percent, respectively—much higher than city population growth (2.4 and 2.0 percent, respectively) as a whole. The four largest cities (with populations more than 4.2 million) collectively have 3.6 million slum dwellers, accounting for 9.1 percent of the total population (Lall, Timmons, and Yu 2009).

Elasticity of housing supply in the formal market appears to be very low, limiting the degree to which the supply can respond to demand increases. The estimated housing supply elasticity is similar to that of Malaysia

and the Republic of Korea, which are considered to have restrictive land regulations (Lall, Timmons, and Yu 2009). Using data for slum formation across Brazilian cities between 1980 and 2000, Da Mata (2006) shows that pro-poor land use regulations like minimum lot size encourage immigration of the poor and increase slum formation. But urban zoning regulations are found to have a positive effect on the growth of formal housing markets and city population. Urban zoning regulations are likely to improve land use efficiency by facilitating timely infrastructure investments both in urban expansion and redevelopment. It is key to identify policies that increase the housing supply relative to population growth and improve the elasticity of housing supply (Lall, Timmons, and Yu 2009).

Land regulations are just one of many exclusionary policies in the hands of local authorities that could lead to growing slums. There is evidence that during the dictatorship localities appeared to withhold services, measured as water connections, to deter in-migration of low-education households (Feler and Henderson 2011). These early strategic interactions—where localities respond to increases in service in other localities by withholding their own service—led to the growth of many unserviced informal housing sectors. The implications of these policies are costly, as catch-up investments are required, and building infrastructure on developed neighborhoods is considerably more costly than greenfield development.

Connecting

Connective investments maintain and enhance cities' competitiveness. Previous connecting efforts seem to have paid off, leading to a well-functioning system of cities. But as Brazil moves toward higher incomes, it will be important to become more competitive. Considerable investments in infrastructure may be necessary. Investments in short distance trips are particularly important.

Coordination across jurisdictions will be key to tackle the challenges in large cities.

Efforts to improve governance of metropolitan areas will also be important to reduce disparities within the largest cities; coordination across jurisdictions would improve efficiency in land use planning as well as provision of basic services.

Notes

1. The Herfindahl- Hirschman Index (HHI) provides a quantitative measure of the importance of a particular sector in a region. When the region is completely specialized, the index approaches one, while if no single sector dominates the region, the index approaches zero.
2. The location quotient, a measure of geographic concentration of an industry, is defined as the ratio of a location's share of the industry's employment to its share of national employment. Values above/less than 1 indicate that the location is relatively more/less specialized in the industry than the national average.
3. Half minimum wage has been used in Brazil to define a poverty line. Households living with less than half minimum wage are considered poor and those living with less than a fourth are considered indigents (PNUD 2003).

References

Da Mata, Daniel, Uwe Deichmann, J. Vernon Henderson, Somik V. Lall, and Hyoung Gun Wang. 2006. "Um Exame dos Padrões de Crescimento das Cidades Brasileiras." Discussion Papers 1155, Instituto de Pesquisa Econômica Aplicada, Brasilia.

———. 2007. "Determinant of City Growth in Brazil." *Journal of Urban Economics* 62: 252–72.

Feler, Leo, and J. Vernon Henderson. 2011. "Exclusionary Policies in Urban Development: Under-Servicing Migrant Households in Brazilian Cities." *Journal of Urban Economics* 69 (3): 253–72.

Lall, Somik V., Christopher Timmins, and Shouyue Yu. 2009. "Connecting Lagging and Leading Regions: The Role of Labor Mobility." Policy Research Working Paper 4843, World Bank, Washington, DC.

PNUD (Programa das Nações Unidas para o Desenvolvimento). 2003. "Atlas do Desenvolvimento Humano no Brasil." Brasilia.

World Bank. 2006. *Brazil—Inputs for a Strategy for Cities: A Contribution with a Focus on Cities and Municipalities.* Report No. 35749-BR. Washington, DC: Latin America and the Caribbean Region, Finance, Private Sector and Infrastructure Management Unit.

CHINA

China embraced the urbanization that accompanied its dramatic economic transformation. Roughly 1 of 10 people in the world is a resident of a Chinese city. The United Nations projects that Chinese urban dwellers will increase from more than 622 million today to more than 1 billion by about 2030. How China manages its urban transformation will have considerable bearing not only for the Chinese economy and society, but for the world at large.

How China is urbanizing

China's urbanization has been characterized by spatial expansion—particularly in large cities. With monopoly powers on urban land supply, municipal governments have had considerable influence on land conversion and use to accommodate people and economic activities. Cities such as Beijing, Shanghai, and Guangzhou have rapidly suburbanized. While population densities are greatest in the city core, population growth or urban expansion is much higher in the fringe areas 30–40 kilometers from the city center.

Spatial expansion has been accompanied by higher land consumption per capita in these big cities, where higher incomes have bid up the demand for land and housing.

Economic prosperity is concentrated in large cities with good access to international markets (map 4.1). Urbanization—particularly urban concentration in the largest cities—has amplified economic progress. Cities with 2.5 million or more people generate 76 percent of urban exports;[1] and 62 percent of overall foreign capital is used in these cities. Proximity to international markets has been the main driver of urbanization and urban success.

The urban economic structure is more complex when looked at closely. For example, big cities tend to generate higher incomes, but there are large variations within each city size

group, likely due to economic geography conditions and other local factors.

While overall poverty reduction has been impressive, the coastal-inland development gap and the rural-urban divide are the two major components of spatial inequality in China. Spatial transformations have stimulated progress in large coastal cities, but many poor people in rural areas and small hinterland cities still need to be connected with prosperity. The rural poor account for 91 percent of the total poor; and western provinces (north and south) account for more than 50 percent, though the western region represents only around 20 percent of the national population (World Bank 2008).

In addition to rural-urban and broad regional divisions, the urban underclass is concentrated in second-tier cities (nonprovincial capitals). The four largest provincial megacities (Beijing, Shanghai, Chongqing, and Tianjin) have the lowest urban disadvantaged rate of around 1 percent. More than 80 percent of the urban underclass lives in prefectural or lower-level cities.

Urban challenges

Rural-urban land use conversion

Rural land can be transformed for urban land use only when the municipal government purchases the land from rural communes. This effectively makes municipal governments the monopoly supplier of urban land in the primary land market.

Since 2001, the focus has shifted from a centrally planned system to a more market-oriented system. Conveyance transactions have started to account for a larger share in the primary market. The government sets principles and procedures to increase transparency.

The rapid outward spread of cities has led to greater concern from the central government over the loss of China's farmlands. The relatively small percentage of arable land (around 14 percent) has amplified this concern, as has the government's longstanding commitment to sustaining food self-sufficiency for security reasons. Although China

---

The China Urbanization Review has been prepared by a team led by Hyoung Gun Wang and comprising Somik V. Lall and Yuanyuan Jiang.

is committed to a strict policy of farmland protection, many local governments rely heavily on off-budget revenues from land lease transactions to fund economic and infrastructure programs.

Labor mobility

Under the *hukou* system, or regulations on household registration, every Chinese is assigned a *hukou* location with either agricultural (rural) or nonagricultural (urban) *hukou* classifications. An agricultural *hukou* provides access to farmland, and a nonagricultural *hukou* provides access to jobs, housing, food, and state-sponsored benefits. Without an urban *hukou,* unregistered migrants cannot have access to basic needs of urban life, including jobs, housing, and public and social services.

As local governments implemented various *hukou* reforms after the 1980s, local *hukou* regulations vary greatly from city to city. In general, it is more difficult to obtain a local *hukou* in a larger city than a smaller one. The *hukou* system is the main barrier limiting rural-urban migration, especially for large cities such as Beijing, Shanghai, and Guangzhou.

Basic services

Recent policy initiatives indicate an increasing government commitment to broader poverty reduction, social protection, and human development. The quality of life in urban and rural areas has improved greatly in the past decade, measured by net income and Engel's coefficient.[2] And the rural-urban difference in the expenditure share on social services (education and health) diminished significantly over 1990–2008. But the income disparity between the urban and rural residents has widened over time.

The overall quality of health services is a cause for concern. There is hardly any improvement, and in some instances it is deteriorating. Local governments' limited capacity to generate fiscal revenues contributes to poor basic services in small cities. More important, urban water infrastructure fails to provide sufficient water and meet ever-increasing urban demand.

MAP 4.1　Economic concentration of GDP, 2007

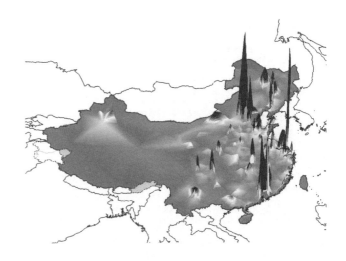

Source: Authors' calculation using Statistical Yearbooks by the National Bureau of Statistics of China.

Connecting cities

Massive infrastructure construction, particularly the national transport network, has largely driven China's economic growth. The national transport network expanded rapidly. From 1990 to 2005, China completed nearly 41,000 kilometers of high-grade tolled expressways comprising the National Trunk Highway System, or the National Expressway Network (NEN). During this period, about 400,000 kilometers of local and township roads were also improved. This expansion was funded by investments upward of $40 billion a year, with about a third allocated to the NEN. The current NEN plan includes 7 corridors radiating from Beijing, 9 north-south corridors, and 18 east-west corridors. The strategy for defining the 7–9–18 plan combined radial and grid patterns to maximize coverage and transport connections.

Despite China's recent efforts to update the transport infrastructure, the logistics industry still needs to improve its efficiency to reduce associated costs. China's expense on logistics accounted for 20 percent of the GDP—much higher than the United States (10 percent), Japan (14 percent), and the European Union (10–13 percent). A logistics performance study ranked China's domestic logistics costs 72 of 150 countries (World Bank 2007).

Connecting neighborhoods within cities

Chinese cities are moving toward motorized transport with rapid growth in the use of private cars and public transport. This is coupled with fast growth in inner suburb and outer suburb trips in large cities, where residential development has been concentrated recently.

Nonmotorized travel, including walking and biking, continues to decline in favor of motorized trips on both public and private modes. Private motorized vehicles are gaining a larger share of travel (Darido, Torres-Montoya, and Mehndiratta 2009). Similar trends can be seen for public transportation and taxis. Nonmotorized travel in big cities—including Beijing, Shanghai, Guangzhou, and Xi'an—has declined well below 50 percent, whereas the majority of residents in small cities travel to work by foot or bicycle. This indicates that each local urban transport policy should be differentiated according to its own city size and development rather than a one-size-fits-all approach.

The average portion of the transportation expenditure to discretionary income in Beijing, Shanghai, and the nation as a whole has risen steadily over the past few years. The proportion that the low-income group spends on transport has grown much faster in Beijing, while Shanghai succeeded in making urban transport inclusive for low-income city residents. Without targeted interventions and investments, low-income urban residents will face greater pressure to manage travel expenditures as cities expand and motorize.

Financing

With the introduction of fiscal contracts in 1988, the central government is no longer responsible for financing local expenditures. Instead, the local government's role expanded from providing public services to financing them as well. Local governments are responsible for a wide spectrum of government functions (box 4.1).[3]

As transfers from the central government are allocated through a revenue-sharing mechanism, rich and big cities receive larger transfers than small cities (Mountfield and Wong 2005). Thus local governments' ability to raise revenues either on- or off-budget is crucial for high-quality public services.

Local governments in larger cities generate disproportionately higher revenues per capita than smaller cities. Residents in large cities

---

BOX 4.1 China's urban infrastructure financing

Debt financing. To fill the gap created by the decline in direct budget spending, local governments have primarily turned to borrowing. In 2001, commercial bank loans accounted for more than 30 percent of infrastructure investment by local governments. The central government strongly encouraged this policy, identifying urban infrastructure investment as a top priority for banks. And this lending was seen as implicitly guaranteed by the central government. The central government also issued infrastructure bonds and passed the proceeds to provincial and local governments as a mix of on-lending and grants.

Marketization. "Marketization" describes the mobilization of capital from the private sector to invest in urban infrastructure. The national planning agency is increasingly calling for this mode of financing to replace the declining share of direct budget financing. There are two key elements to the marketization financing.

First, marketization financing earns proceeds from land leasing—that is, the sale of leasing rights owned by the local government to private developers. Leasing rights, typically for 40–70 years, are sold up-front as a cash transaction.

Second, the local governments are increasingly moving toward "privatizing" existing infrastructure assets. This can be viewed as a way of attracting private capital to help finance new infrastructure projects.

enjoy better access to high-quality public services, as their local governments can generate more revenues in both absolute and relative terms.

Looking ahead

China's urbanization should amplify the pace of economic prosperity and enhance living conditions across the country's vast landscape. Public policy and investment need to generate win-wins for urban efficiency and social inclusion. As other parts of the urban system start benefiting from more prosperity, the management of urbanization and urban land consumption is likely to have considerable bearing on urban productivity, mobility, and sustainability.

Notes

1. As of 2007 (Statistical Yearbook).
2. The Engel's coefficient serves as a measure of the standard of living in a country. It measures the percentage of a household's expenditure on food relative to its total spending. A low coefficient indicates a high standard of living.
3. Subnational government administration; local capital construction; basic local services (water supply and distribution, local and regional roads and highways, wastewater collection and treatment, garbage collection

and disposal, urban gas supply, mass transit); maintenance, repair, and operation of urban infrastructure; management of local state owned enterprises; expenditure for agriculture production; primary and secondary schooling and a large portion of higher education; health clinics and hospitals; price subsides; poverty reduction; protection of laid-off workers from state owned enterprises; cultural and heritage protection; local and regional economic development; and physical planning.

References

Darido, Georges, Mariana Torres-Montoya, and Shomik Mehndiratta. 2009. "Urban Transport and CO_2 Emissions: Some Evidence from Chinese Cities." Working Paper, World Bank, Washington, DC.

Mountfield, Edward, and Christine P. Wong. 2005. "Public Expenditure on the Frontline: Toward Effective Management by Subnational Governments." In *East Asia Decentralizes: Making Local Government Work*. Washington, DC: World Bank.

National Bureau of Statistics of China. Statistical Yearbooks. Several years. Beijing.

World Bank. 2007. *Connecting to Compete 2007: Trade Logistics in the Global Economy*. Washington, DC: World Bank.

———. 2008. *World Development Report 2009: Reshaping Economic Geography*. Washington, DC: World Bank.

COLOMBIA

Seventy-five percent of Colombians live in cities. Bogotá, home to 7 million, is Colombia's largest city, with 18,000 people per square kilometer—the densest in the western hemisphere. Together with Cali, Medellín, and Barranquilla, the largest cities account for 30 percent of the country's population and a high proportion of its jobs. At the other end of the spectrum lie 927 municipalities with fewer than 20,000 people, dispersed across the national landscape. How city leaders manage the urban system will impact Colombia's chances of transitioning from a middle-income to a high-income country.

How Colombia is urbanizing

Colombia, as much of Latin America, has enjoyed positive economic growth in the past few years, mitigating the potential adverse consequences of the global financial crisis. These gains came on the back of high commodity prices, improvements in macroeconomic and financial management, diversification of trading partners—particularly through stronger links with China—and safer integration into international financial markets (World Bank 2011). While Colombia is still highly dependent on commodities, urban activities are central to its growth. Urban activities have contributed to more than 50 percent of GDP growth over the past four decades.[1]

Strengthening cities' contribution can help mitigate the risks inherent to commodity-intensive economies and support the move

from a commodity-driven economic system to a stronger resource-based manufacturing structure and then toward knowledge-intensive industries (Sinnott, Nash, and de la Torre 2010). High-income countries such as Australia, Canada, the Scandinavian countries, and the United States have evolved similarly (Blomström and Meller 1991; De Ferranti and others 2002). Almost 80 percent of Colombians live in urban areas, where unemployment rates are above 12 percent—among the highest in the region.

Urban challenges

What key drivers will enable Colombia's urban system to cash in on its growth dividend? The Colombia Urbanization Review focuses on three priorities: enhancing planning coordination at a regional and metropolitan scale, deepening economic connections across cities, and fostering efficiency and innovation in how cities finance themselves.

Enhancing coordination for better planning

Colombia is one of the most decentralized countries in Latin America. More than 1,000 municipal governments have identical responsibilities for basic infrastructure service delivery, land use and economic development planning, and provision of social services. But the footprint of urbanization is frequently greater than municipal boundaries. The metropolitan area of Bogotá covers seven municipal jurisdictions (Bogotá, La Calera, Chía, Cota, Funza, Mosquera, and Soacha) and has a population of about 8.1 million. This occupation pattern is not primarily sprawl—Bogotá is one of the most densely populated cities in the world. And this spatial pattern is not unique to Bogotá. Firms and households in other large and medium cities are increasingly spilling across the boundaries of core municipalities, driven by natural economic forces including access to affordable land.

Metropolitan areas in Colombia face crippling inertia and bottlenecks in planning land use and strategic investment. The

The Colombia Urbanization Review has been prepared by a team led by Taimur Samad (task team leader) and Nancy Lozano-Gracia (co–task team leader), comprising Bernadette Baird-Zars, Henry Jewell, Yoonhee Kim, Somik V. Lall, Alexandra Panman, Alejandro Rodriguez, and Hyoung Gun Wang. Consultants whose reports served as inputs for this work include: Francisco Perdomo and Pablo Roda; Francisco Rodriquez; Oscar Arboleda, Juan Benavides, Mauricio Olivera, and Claudia Patricia Quintero; and Nicolas Ronderos and Robert Yaro. The main counterpart for this report in the government of Colombia was the National Planning Department.

benefits of coordinated land use include the development of productive and logistics infrastructure and of structural drainage and flood protection infrastructure and the efficient spatial organization of economic activities. Despite the benefits that may arise from interjurisdictional coordination, many political economy challenges discourage coordinated services and planning across administrative boundaries.

In decentralized systems like Colombia, local administrators and politicians face strong disincentives to coordinate regional actions. Resistance often emerges to aggregation or "clawing back" of power and responsibility from the municipal level.

Deepening economic connections

Colombia's geography poses serious challenges for interregional transport. As early as 1927, studies have noted that the natural and economic geography poses a particular challenge for transport in Colombia (Renner 1927; Stokes 1967). Many cities are dispersed across mountainous terrain and far from coastal ports. Bogotá, the country's primary production center, is more than a day's drive from the Atlantic or Pacific coasts, where agricultural products for export, fossil fuels, and raw materials are concentrated. Because many imports and exports are processed in maritime ports, freight travels long distances in Colombia. A 2006 study showed that freight distances in Colombia were almost three times those in Brazil and Chile, five times those in Malaysia, and six times those in Argentina, China, and the Republic of Korea.

In Colombia, physical distances are exacerbated by economic distances. Costs for freight transport on domestic roads from Bogotá to the Atlantic are about $94 per ton, while international maritime transport to the United States is about $75 per ton. Moving products from Bogotá to Barranquilla costs $88 per ton, and Bogotá to Buenaventura $54 per ton. Shipping goods from Cartagena or Buenaventura to Rotterdam or Shanghai is about $60 per ton—that is, less than the transport costs from Bogotá to the ports

for the Atlantic and slightly higher for the Pacific. Logistic costs are also high.

Fostering efficiency and innovation in financing

Smaller municipalities are highly dependent on transfers from the national government. About 70 percent of the revenues of small municipalities come from national transfers, compared with about 30 percent for the largest municipalities. Heavy reliance on transfers may weaken accountability, as the political costs of raising funds are borne at the national level and not directly where they are spent. This is important because service quality remains a major challenge in Colombia.

Earmarking transfers for spending in particular sectors may not be sufficient to ensure quality improvements without mechanisms to measure the investments' effectiveness. Excessive reliance on earmarking could also encourage fiscal laziness, as municipalities lack the incentive to raise revenue and direct it to specific local needs. And evidence suggests that heavy reliance on transfers can lead to inefficient spending.

While municipal tax collection has risen with decentralization and administrative reforms across all categories of cities, small and medium cities have not kept pace with larger cities in their ability to increase local revenues. Municipal capacity to raise property taxes is closely connected to the efficiency of the cadastral system: there is a positive correlation between property tax revenue and the cadastral system's accuracy. Only Bogotá, Medellín, and Cali have independent cadastre offices, and all others are handled at the national level. Large cities have more comprehensive land cadastres. Bogotá has attained 100 percent registration of land. By contrast, only 43 percent of rural areas are included within the national registration system.

Looking ahead

Coordinating

The government has an important role in aligning incentives and fostering coordination among local governments. International experience demonstrates that national governments and urban areas have successfully responded to changing conditions by reforming interjurisdictional coordination arrangements. The role of national government is to build a framework and create the right incentives for coordination. This may include strengthening metropolitan governance structures through building capacity, expanding metropolitan competencies, regulating and promoting cooperation structures, and developing coordinated projects between the national and regional governments. Financial incentives can also promote horizontal coordination.

Efforts to increase coordination across jurisdictions are particularly timely in light of new legal reforms. The new law regulating spatial planning—Ley Orgánica de Ordenamiento Territorial—responds to the need to develop a clear institutional framework to support the aggregation of municipal functions and coordination between territorial entities. The law opens spaces for voluntary collaboration in institutional interjurisdictional arrangements and enables the formation of organizational entities (commissions) to collaborate on territorial planning issues. But it does establish clearly defined coordination responsibilities. Its pending regulation will present a critical opportunity for the government to ensure the new legal framework has the ability to claw back excessive decentralization.

Connecting

Lowering transport costs will catalyze growth and improve overall efficiency across the system of cities in Colombia. The Colombia Urbanization Review identified two possible ways to reduce costs: improvements to intermodality and investments in specific corridors that will face high congestion as soon as 2020.

A preliminary simulation analyzing the competitiveness of three modes (truck, rail, and waterways) suggests that more competition across modes would bring considerable cost savings. The simulation suggests that, given limited access to marine terminals,

trucking is the most cost-effective mode for distances less than 300 kilometers. For medium distances, rail is the most cost-effective, and for distances beyond 700 kilometers river transport is the most cost-effective. Distances from Bogotá to the Atlantic coast are roughly 1,000 kilometers, suggesting a large benefit from greater modal diversity.

And from a demand-side perspective, the two main corridors identified as medium-term priorities are the route along the eastern mountain chain, connecting Bogotá to the Atlantic Coast ports, and the route connecting the highlands to the Pacific ports (from Bogotá to Buenaventura). Note that the demand models used in this assessment factor in today's ongoing pipeline investments (such as *Ruta del Sol*, along the Bogotá-Atlantic Coast Corridor). Even with these investments factored in, projected growth in demand will cause substantial congestion on these routes as early as 2020.

Reduced transport costs resulting from connective investments and competition across modes will likely alter the distribution of trade across the system of cities. It will also open new opportunities for places and products that were constrained by high costs. Rather than focusing on picking winners and losers, national policy should aim to reduce market and government failures—here the market failures, related to infrastructure provision, that impede trade among Colombian cities and between them and the rest of the world.

Financing

A strong push is required to strengthen the fiscal fundamentals for small and medium cities. This might be done through increased capacity building in municipal fiscal management, strengthened local cadastral systems, and the structuring of fiscal and performance incentives within the national transfer system. In the face of considerable infrastructure finance gaps, medium and large cities must find new ways to finance urban infrastructure. Cities will require diversified strategies, including increasing access to municipal bonds and credit markets, elaborating existing land-based financing instruments, and accessing municipal development funds and specialized financial intermediaries. Colombia is a leader in land-based financing instruments in Latin America. But these innovative land-based financing instruments have had limited penetration beyond Colombia's large cities, where they have also run into capacity and technical constraints. Medium and large cities should also create new instruments for infrastructure financing such as tradable development rights, land sales and leases, tax increment financing, and private-public partnerships for urban redevelopment and renovation.

The national government has a broader role in supporting the financial efforts of cities. More systematic data on expenditures as well as close monitoring and evaluation would clarify the impact of specific conditions, such as earmarking, on efficiency of investment. The government may also consider developing and deepening efforts to support fiscal capacity at the municipal level, targeting assistance strategically within the "system of cities" approach. Efforts may include creating programs to develop municipal cadastres in medium cities, targeting technical assistance across the system of cities in investment planning and fiscal management, and working with medium cities on municipal creditworthiness.

The government may also analyze and develop greater performance-based incentives within the Sistema General de Participaciones framework to improve the efficiency and effectiveness of the transfers and overall municipal investment. And the government has a unique opportunity to structure the regional development fund within the context of the Royalties Law (Ley de Regalias) to create the right incentives for strategic investment planning and development. Allowing this fund to be a formula-driven transfer to departments

would merely reproduce past errors in the royalties system. The royalties fund for regional development should be designed with strong performance-based criteria, filter investment priorities through a "system of cities" technical framework, and create incentives for effective cooperation across municipalities and between departments.

Note

1. Urban activities include commerce, restaurants, hotels, manufacture, financing, and other services. Urbanization Review calculations are based on a moving average of the component of the economy's growth rate contributed by purely urban activities.

References

Blomström, Magnus, and Patricio Meller. 1991. "Issues for Development: Lessons from Scandinavia and Latin American Development." In *Diverging Paths: Comparing a Century of Scandinavian and Latin American Development*, ed. Magnus Blomström and Patricio Meller. Washington, DC: Inter-American Development Bank.

de Ferranti, David, Guillermo E. Perry, Daniel Lederman, and William F. Maloney. 2002. *From Natural Resources to the Knowledge Economy: Trade and Job Quality*. Latin American and Caribbean Studies. Washington, DC: World Bank.

Renner, G.T., Jr. 1927. "Colombia's Internal Development." *Economic Geography* 3 (2): 259–64.

Sinnott, Emily, John Nash, and Augusto de la Torre. 2010. *Natural Resources in Latin America and the Caribbean beyond Booms and Busts?* Washington, DC: World Bank.

Stokes, Charles J. 1967. "The Freight Transport System of Colombia, 1959." *Economic Geography* 43 (1): 71–90.

World Bank. 2011. "LAC Success Put to the Test." Office of the Chief Economist, Latin America and the Caribbean, World Bank, Washington, DC.

INDIA

Identifying options for accommodating urban expansion is gaining importance in India's policy discourse. Since 2001, another 90 million people have joined the urban ranks, and 250 million more are projected by 2030. The challenge—as well as the opportunity—is extremely high population densities in and around the largest metropolitan areas. Population densities in the 50-kilometer vicinity of the largest metropolises average 2,450 people per square kilometer. And a third of India's new towns were "born" in a 50-kilometer neighborhood of existing cities with more than one million people.[1]

If these trends are any indication of the future, much of India's urbanization challenge will be to transform land use and expand infrastructure in its largest cities and neighboring suburbs—places that are not pristine or greenfield but already support 9 percent of the country's population and provide 18 percent of employment on 1 percent of its land area. So far, high population densities have not been accompanied by commensurate substitution between scarce land and durable capital or built-up area.

How urbanization is managed has implications for economic efficiency and spatial equity. For economic efficiency, it is important to learn where the transformation is occurring and whether productivity gains through agglomeration economies are being adequately tapped. Are policy distortions stymying such benefits, and can specific reforms reduce the inefficiencies? For spatial equity, it is important to learn whether the benefits of the transformation are spreading geographically and whether policies can help spread economic activities.

The India Urbanization Review was prepared by a core team led by Tara Vishwanath, consisting of David Dowall, Somik V. Lall, Nancy Lozano-Gracia, Siddharth Sharma, Eugenia Suarez, Hyoung Gun Wang, and Cheryl Young. The policy discussion in this report was framed following extensive discussions with the Planning Commission and the Ministries of Urban Development and Housing and Urban Poverty Alleviation.

How India is urbanizing

An assessment of India's urbanization highlights considerable stability in the spatial distribution of people and jobs. One would expect rapid economic concentration in large metropolitan areas with good market access following economic liberalization, as in China during the 1980s and in other Asian countries following economic integration. But India's metropolitan areas have not gained discernibly in economic activity. True, the seven largest such areas have the highest concentration of economic activities that benefit from urbanization economies—information and communication technology (ICT), machine tools, rapidly growing export manufacturing, and supporting services. But these metropolitan areas have been stagnant in recent years (figure 4.4). Over 1993–2006, they did not increase their overall shares in national employment—not even in industries that typically benefit from agglomeration economies, such as ICT and high-tech manufacturing.

The cross-country experience, that metropolitan concentration increases until per capita income levels of $7,000–$10,000 are reached, suggests that the liberalization of industrial investment in the 1990s should have led to greater economic concentration in India's metropolitan areas. The stagnancy of these metropolitan areas in recent years points to three overlapping scenarios.

First, industry in India has not grown rapidly, thus reducing the demand for urban agglomerations that can provide localization and urbanization economies. But this is not entirely convincing as India has developed niche markets in ICT services and specialized manufacturing that it trades with the rest of the world. And there has been considerable growth in low-end manufacturing that is consumed and traded internally. By looking at differences between Karnataka and Tamil Nadu—India's high-growth states—it is becoming clear that economic geography has a role to play in influencing specializations across urban areas.

Second, India's cities have some of the most restrictive rules on conversion of land

FIGURE 4.4   **Employment growth in metropolitan cores and periphery, by sector, 1998–2005**

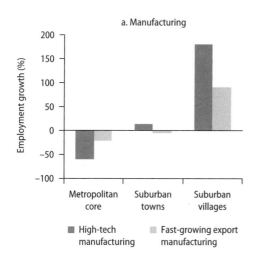

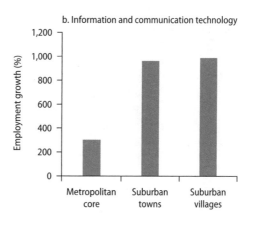

Sources: Ministry of Statistics and Programme Implementation 1998 and 2005.
Note: The metropolitan core is an area with a 10 kilometer radius, centered on the main metropolis. Suburban towns include urban areas 10–50 kilometers from the metropolitan core. Suburban villages include rural areas in the same vicinity. These figures are averages for the seven largest metropolitan areas (Mumbai, Delhi, Bangalore, Kolkata, Chennai, Hyderabad, and Ahmedabad).

for urban use and on the intensity with which land can be used to accommodate industry and commerce. For example, even though the standard practice in cities with limited land is to raise the permitted floor space index (FSI) over time to accommodate growth, the Municipal Corporation of Greater Mumbai lowered the permitted FSI to 1.33 in 1991 (World Bank 2008). In this otherwise liberalized policy environment, stringent regulation on development densities is pushing businesses and people out of urban centers. The constraints on land use are also making housing expensive, pricing out poor and middle-class households from urban centers.

Third, all metropolitan suburbs—whether officially classified as rural or urban—are experiencing an industrial boom. At 41 percent, the pace of manufacturing employment growth is fastest in the rural areas adjacent to the largest metropolitan areas. Even though high-tech and other emerging manufacturing industries are moving away from the centers of metropolitan areas, they are relocating to the suburbs and peripheries of these same cities, rather than to smaller cities. And although metropolitan suburbanization is a

worldwide phenomenon, it usually happens at middle to advanced stages of development.[2] India's early suburbanization suggests that the overall stagnancy of metropolitan areas is partly due to firms being pushed out of the cores. The growth of metropolitan suburbs is possibly a reaction to these draconian land policy regulations. But the journey to the suburbs is costly for firms and workers. Transport costs for freight are among the highest between the metropolitan core and its periphery, and infrastructure access and quality of water, electricity, and sanitation is much worse at the urban periphery relative to the core.

Urban challenges

Rigid land use policies
Urbanization brings higher demand for land, and a problem arises when land is scarce where it is needed most. India lacks many of the institutions—such as a transparent system to convert land use, a clear definition of property rights, a robust system of land and property valuation, and a strong judicial system to address public concerns—that are

needed to facilitate land markets and make it easier to accommodate land transactions and land use changes. While stronger institutions governing land use conversion, land valuation, and property rights definition and adjudication emerge, and land markets mature over time, India may want to look at alternative options for the short and medium term. Land readjustment is gaining acceptance as an alternative to land acquisition as it has many advantages for land assembly. Essentially a participatory tool, land readjustment to a great extent avoids the public discontent and protests that land acquisition may generate.

Sprawl and escalating property prices

Managing densities within cities is another challenge in accommodating urban expansion, as is financing urban expansion and city renewal. Urban regulations such as FSIs limit densification in Indian cities, capping densities at levels much below international good practice. And India's cities have blanket FSIs that cover large areas, thus missing opportunities to strategically increase density around infrastructure networks. Granularity in FSI design and coordination of land use to exploit infrastructure placement is the bedrock of good urban planning (as in Seoul and Singapore).

Commuting and freight transport

While urban land and building regulations limit densities in metropolitan cores and push people and firms to the outskirts, deficient connections are exacerbating these constraints. If a good transport system is in place, people can make efficient tradeoffs between how much they consume and its quality, and the distance they travel to work. But congestion presents a major challenge for Indian cities. Narrow roads, combined with pervasive growth of private car ownership, lead to motorized journey speeds in all cities that are barely faster than riding a bicycle. While motorization is on the rise, public transport has not been able to serve the expanding mass of urban commuters. Discussions with urban transport experts suggest that even

though several initiatives increase the supply of public transport, limited integration with other modes of transport and land use planning reduces its use.

Just as urban transport is key to connecting people with jobs, an adequate logistics infrastructure is needed for city businesses to reach local and regional markets. Market access provides incentives for firms to increase production scale and specialize. But as businesses suburbanize, they face higher costs to connect with urban markets. Freight costs between metropolitan cores and their peripheries are as high as Rs 5.2 ton per kilometer ($0.12)—twice the national average of Rs 2.6 and more than five times the cost to move products in countries such as the United States. Much of the high transport costs are due to use of smaller and older trucks as well as a higher share of empty backhauls without a return load. Trucks on these routes clock about 25,000 kilometers a year, a fourth of what they need to be economically viable. Logistics management systems and collaboration and consolidation with competing truckers and trucking associations can help internalize the network externalities and reduce metropolitan freight costs.

Spatial disparities in access to basic services

Access to and quality of basic services both matter for living standards of households and performance of firms. India has a long way to go to provide universal access to basic services. Access to services such as sewerage and drainage facilities worsen as city size decreases, with small towns and rural areas suffering from the lowest access levels. Two factors drive these differences: fragmented institutional responsibilities between state and central governments, and regulations that keep tariffs low and do not allow utilities to be financially sustainable, making them unable to expand services.

Looking ahead

Planning

To accommodate urban expansion, India needs to change its urban planning "License

Raj." Getting urban planning right is essential for economic prosperity. Urban planning systems across the country limit urban expansion, redevelopment, modernization, and the repurposing of older, inefficient areas. In setting out to relax these constraints, Indian policy makers could embark on "big bang" reforms such as those in Hong Kong SAR, China; the Republic of Korea, and Singapore—which followed a big push model of "managed urbanization" led by a strong and often intrusive state. But this approach could face high political and social risks. Another option—which may be more conducive to India's democratic and federal system—is to pursue an incremental model of experimentation focusing on a few areas (such as infrastructure corridors and neighborhoods) and then scaling up based on community-level consensus building. This will also allow for learning from alternative approaches and lead to capacity building at the local level.

Responsibility for urban reforms

Who is responsible for implementing urban reforms in a federal country where national, state, and municipal jurisdictions overlap? Some very local- or neighborhood-level decisions on densification and infrastructure planning are often decided at the state level; and the guidelines on land valuation are concurrently handled by national and state governments with some inputs from the districts (not the municipalities). Similarly, urban basic services such as water supply are often provided by state-level public health and engineering departments, often missing out on economies of scale and scope that could come from differentiating service options across settlements with varying densities.

Metropolitan-wide horizontal coordination

Beyond the implementation challenges of vertical coordination, the rapidly increasing spatial footprint or suburbanization of India's urban areas is creating a disconnect between what is "urban" and what is "municipal," calling for metropolitanwide horizontal coordination. International experience points to several criteria for designing metropolitan

governance structures, including efficiency in exploiting economies of scale and ability to reduce negative spillovers across municipal boundaries, equity in sharing costs and benefits of services across the metropolitan area, accountability for decision making, and local responsiveness. Agencies such as the Bangalore Metropolitan Region Development Authority and the Mumbai Metropolitan Region Development Authority have been instituted to facilitate metropolitan-wide functional and investment coordination. But the jury is still out on the effectiveness of these institutions in performing their intended roles and of their ability to manage efficiency, equity, and accountability across metropolitan areas.

Notes

1. Of the 1,108 new towns "born" between 1991 and 2001, 35 percent were in urban fringe areas within 50 kilometers of medium and large cities of more than 1 million people.
2. For Brazil, see Townroe (1981) and Hansen (1983). For the Republic of Korea, see Chun and Lee (1985) and Henderson, Lee, and Lee (1999). Gregory Ingram (1998) highlights that the general trend of urban development included dispersal from the center to the periphery of both population and employment, with the largest metropolitan areas converging to decentralized and multiple subcentered areas.

References

Chun, Dong Hoon, and Kyu Sik Lee. 1985. "Changing Location Patterns of Population and Employment in the Seoul Region." Discussion paper UDD65, World Bank, Washington, DC.

Hansen, Eric R. 1983. "Why Do Firms Locate Where They Do?" Discussion paper UDD25, World Bank, Washington, DC.

Henderson, J. Vernon, T. Lee, and J-Y Lee. 1999. "Externalities and Industrial Deconcentration under Rapid Growth." Brown University, Providence, RI.

Ingram, Gregory K. 1998. "Patterns of Metropolitan Development: What Have We Learned?" *Urban Studies* 35 (7): 1019–35.

Ministry of Statistics and Programme Implementation. 1988. "Economic Census 1988: All India Report." Central Statistical Organisation, New Delhi.

——. 2005. "Provisional Results of Economic Census 2005: All India Report." Central Statistical Organisation, New Delhi.

Townroe, Peter. 1981. "Location Factors in the Decentralization of Industry: A Survey of Metropolitan São Paulo." Staff working paper 517, World Bank, Washington, DC.

World Bank. 2008. *World Development Report 2009: Reshaping Economic Geography.* Washington, DC: World Bank.

INDONESIA

The spatial structure of urban growth and development in Indonesia will shape economic growth over the next 15 years, determine the quality of life for urban dwellers, and define the competitiveness of Indonesia's cities. To foster productive clusters of economic activity, the government of Indonesia needs to encourage efficient urban spatial structures, appropriate and timely investments in critical large-scale infrastructure in cities, spatially comprehensive basic services, effective urban management, stronger institutional capacity, and proactive horizontal and vertical coordination of local government actions.

Urbanization is a path-dependent process. Once a city is built, the constructed areas, along with the institutional relations that now manage the city, become increasingly locked-in. The most important task is to engage in proactive planning and management of the city in order to leverage the opportunities generated by agglomeration economies.

By 2025, more than two-thirds of the country's population will be urban. This presents a major opportunity: urbanization can boost regional economic growth and create vibrant cities and metropolitan areas. Urbanization and the agglomeration economies that it generates will be central to Indonesia's development as a middle-income country. If managed properly, urbanization can generate the productivity gains, rising incomes, and economic opportunities needed to support the growing middle-income population.

The Indonesia Urbanization Review was prepared by a team led by Peter Ellis, and included Rumayya Batubara, Arish Dastur, Jennifer Day, David Dowall, Blane Lewis, Harun al-Rasyid Lubis, Edy Priyono, Arlan Rahman, Arief Ramadhian, Wilmar Salim, Rulli Setiawan, Renata Simatupang, Thalyta E. Yuwono, and the Urban and Regional Development Institute. Ira Marina provided excellent logistical support to the team and formatted the report. Country counterparts included Bappenas, the Ministry of Transportation, and representatives of the governments of Jakarta, Surabaya, Medan, and Makassar.

Urbanization in Indonesia will continue to be rapid. In absolute terms, the country is expected to add 56 million people to its urban areas over the next four decades. While demographic and economic concentrations around the Jakarta metropolitan region, and more generally across Java and on Bali, will continue to dominate the country's economy, urbanization is also accelerating in the country's medium-size cities (map 4.2).

How Indonesia is urbanizing

Over the past 20 years, Jakarta has done well despite an influx of residents and serious infrastructure challenges. Surabaya's per capita growth in gross regional domestic product (GRDP) has been slightly weaker, as it did not fully recover from the 1997 crisis, but its growth has been steady since 2003. Medium-size cities have experienced the strongest per capita growth in GRDP, along with strong to moderate population growth. Small cities have performed the weakest, with declines in population and per capita GRDPs. Trends in land, population, infrastructure, investment climate, and economic sector data indicate that the medium-size cities have managed to leverage urbanization for economic growth very well.

Population growth is most rapid in the suburban ring of the metropolitan areas.

MAP 4.2   Economic density is dominant in Java

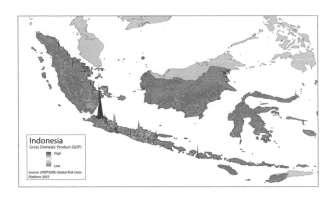

Source: GIS processing World Bank DECRG, Washington, DC, extrapolation UNEP/GRID-Geneva and team elaborations.

More than 70 percent of all urban population growth between 1996 and 2007 took place in the suburban areas of multidistrict metropolitan regions. This fact points to two phenomena: first, many metropolitan regions are gradually deconcentrating their centers as they grow into their peripheries; and second, this expansion cuts across multiple jurisdictions, often with conflicting interests. This requires mechanisms that optimize and coordinate development at a scale more complex and much larger than the city core.

Urban challenges

Land markets

Land markets are constraining the economic development of cities. Local and provincial governments need to enable and manage dynamic land markets. This is possibly one of the biggest bottlenecks Indonesia faces as it urbanizes. Land acquisition processes based on government valuations of land are lengthy and cumbersome, causing long delays and relaying costs to projects and infrastructure construction.

Except for Medan, metropolitan regions are sprawling as real estate developers and businesses find it easier, cheaper, and faster to develop projects in outlying areas. This also follows the international patterns of decentralization of manufacturing. These trends indicate that metropolitan areas are rapidly expanding into outlying areas, and as a consequence, driving population density downward (Firman 2000). Currently, three phenomena are apparent in Indonesia's metropolitan areas: many metro regions are gradually deconcentrating their centers as they grow into their peripheries; periphery areas need to be prepared to receive industry—and this expansion spans across multiple jurisdictions, often with conflicting interests. The data on urban land use and population, when combined with GRDP, clearly illustrate the strong and positive correlation between economic density (GRDP per urban land area) and productivity (GRDP per capita).

Infrastructure and service delivery

Growth in the larger metropolitan areas is also constrained by a lack of large-scale investments and within-city challenges in infrastructure delivery. Access to basic services—clean water, sanitation, electricity, and roads—are generally limited and unequally distributed across regions. About 55 percent of households in Indonesia have access to safe drinking water, but only 15 percent comes from piped water. Access to safe drinking water is higher in urban areas (78 percent) than rural (49 percent). Perpamsi (Association for Local Water Utilities Providers) recorded that 403 local governments (*kota/kabupaten*) out of almost 500 local governments have piped water facilities, but the outreach of the service is still very limited.[1]

While access to clean water and sanitation is limited, access to electricity is relatively higher. Almost 98 percent of urban households used electricity from Perusahaan Listrik Negara (PLN, the state electricity company), while the national rate reached 89 percent. However, this rate varies across the region, as there are provinces with less than 50 percent access to electricity.[2]

Coordination

Lack of coordination greatly affects metropolitan regions that need coordinated land use and spatial planning to foster economic efficiency. With most new urbanization taking place outside central cities—DKI Jakarta, Surabaya, Makassar, Bandung, and others—metropolitan areas cannot effectively plan for future growth or develop budgeting mechanisms to finance needed infrastructure. In some cases, infrastructure investments are not coordinated and road projects stop at district or provincial boundaries. In others, independently developed urban land use plans do not consider the economic transformations in a region, and land use is not structured to foster economic development and boost economic development. This may be one of the most significant factors holding back the development of some of the largest secondary cities.

Transportation

Because of its uniquely archipelagic geography, Indonesia requires an extensive system of maritime ports that are efficiently managed and well connected with urban and rural regions. It is important to invest in water-based transport systems and reduce shipping costs to foster interregional trade.

Looking at the split between transportation modes, however, it is clear that Indonesia has not begun to make greater use of water-based transport systems. Improving both terrestrial and maritime transportation by lowering costs and improving the quality and timeliness of goods and people movement will generate manifold benefits: increased economic integration between regions as well as opportunities to develop supply chains between small, medium, and large cities. Highway construction and maintenance has not kept pace with the country's need to develop strong links with regions.

Looking ahead

Planning

The government needs to fully implement its laws and regulations regarding intergovernmental coordination and metropolitan-scale management of spatial planning, as the lack of intergovernmental coordination is hampering effective spatial planning. District plans are not well aligned with those of contiguous districts, and they are not consistent with the plans of their provinces.

National laws and regulations for the preparation of local (district and provincial) plans should be amended to incorporate infrastructure capital investment programs needed for spatial plan implementation. In the case studies done for this project, we encountered numerous cases where planning was not integrated with infrastructure and financing programs. Part of this limitation is due to unclear legislation, lack of compliance, and limited local capacity to link spatial and infrastructure planning with financial programming. Spatial plans do not appear to fully inform the financial budgeting process of local government agencies.

Complex land rights systems hinder economic development. In the public sector, the costly and time-consuming processes to acquire rights-of-way for infrastructure projects impede construction. Private sector entities are more efficient in land acquisition because they are more flexible and realistic with compensation, but the complexity of the acquisition process drives them to suburban areas were land parcels are larger and, therefore, fewer transactions are typically needed. This promotes fragmented urban development and undermines agglomeration economies and urban revitalization. Systems of guided urbanization, such as land pooling and readjustment, might be part of the broader solution.

The government needs a multifaceted strategy for managing urbanization to further leverage regional growth. Indonesia's urban development strategy needs to be focused along two dimensions. First, it must make spatial planning and investment priorities between tiers of government—national, provincial, and local—more consistent. Second, it must stratify local governments along size characteristics: the two largest metropolitan regions, second-tier metropolitan areas, rapidly agglomerating medium-size cities, and small cities. Urban trends need to be linked with the Economic Transformation Master Plan.

Consistency between spatial plans and investments needs to improve. This requires coordinating spatial planning between levels of government and among districts comprising metropolitan areas, so that plans and investment priorities are more closely aligned with investment priorities. Investment plans for large-scale infrastructure also need to take into account the impact on urban land markets. Greater investment is needed in critical infrastructure (electrical power, transit, surface and maritime transportation networks, and basic services). For example, industrial and business and consumer services districts need to be developed and provided with better transportation accessibility to residential zones.

Connecting

The government needs to connect rapidly agglomerating metropolitan and medium-size cities. These cities have adequate infrastructure and do not suffer from poor spatial structure, but they need more and better infrastructure and connections with major centers and ports. As these cities continue to agglomerate, they should maintain their capital investment programs. Sound spatial planning and land management can help these cities enhance productivity, and regional transportation investments can provide an additional boost.

For Java and Sumatra, the government should consider constructing trans-Java and trans-Sumatra highways to improve the efficiency of surface transportation. A trans-Java corridor would create a strong link between Jakarta and Surabaya, as well as links in secondary cities such as Bandung, Semarang, and Yogyakarta.

Financing

Local governments that are urbanizing need to increase both the level and effectiveness of their capital expenditures, or else risk severely constraining economic growth. The capital expenditures of local governments have a significant and positive influence on district economic growth. Local governments that are relatively more urbanized or have relatively larger urban populations (or both) spend less on capital projects than other local governments. Capital expenditure needs to be increased in more urbanized local governments.

Notes

1. Among them, 383 providers are PDAM (*Perusahaan Daerah Air Minum*, local water utilities provider), 10 are private companies, and another 10 are institutions under the Public Works Office.
2. The electrification rate according to BPS (the Central Statistics Agency) is higher than the rate published by PLN (62.4 percent), but the director of PLN had confirmed the validity of BPS' data (*Jurnas* 2010).

References

Firman, Tom. 2000. "Rural to Urban Land Conversion in Indonesia during Boom and Bust Periods." *Land Use Policy* 17 (1): 13–20.

Jurnas. 2010. "Dirut PLN: Angka Elektrifikasi Versi BPS Jangan Jadikan PLN Berpuas Diri." December 8. www.jurnas.com/news/15014/ Dirut_PLN:_Angka_Elektrifikasi_Versi_BPS_ Jangan_Jadikan_PLN_Berpuas_Diri/193/ Ekonomi.

THE REPUBLIC OF KOREA

Already at an advanced stage of urbanization, the Republic of Korea differs from the other case studies in this report. Through coordinated planning and connecting policies, Korea successfully managed its journey from incipient to advanced urbanization.

Korea has had rapid economic growth since the 1960s, attracting considerable interest from the rest of the world. Through the 1950s, Korea was so poor that people had trouble securing even one meal a day. In 1962, its per capita gross national income was only $76, and total national exports were $55 million.

To address economic development and urbanization, Korea's government implemented the Five-Year National Economic Development Plans and the National Territory Comprehensive Plans. Due to these plans, Korea began a journey of economic progress with an average economic growth of 22.6 percent in the late 1960s. High economic growth continued until the 2000s, when Korea had the 15th largest GDP. Korea joined the Organization for Economic Cooperation and Development in 1996 and hosted the G-20 Summit in 2010. How did Korea do it?

How Korea urbanized

Korea's urbanization can be divided into three stages: incipient (1920s to 1960), intermediate (1960 to 1990), and advanced (1990s and on).

Incipient urbanization

The rate of urbanization in 1920 was 4.86 percent, but it rapidly increased to 23.8 percent by 1944. After the Korean War in the

The Korea Urbanization Review is based on the report *Urbanization and Urban Policies in Korea*, which was produced by Korea Research Institute for Human Settlements (KRIHS). The authors of this report include Jaegil Park (lead author), Daejong Kim, Eunnan Kim, Keuntae Kim Yongseok Ko, and Keunhyun Park at KRIHS. The Korea Urbanization Review was prepared in close collaboration between Somik V. Lall and Hyoung Gun Wang from the World Bank and KRIHS in 2010.

1950s, social and political chaos frequently broke out, leading to a high concentration of population in urban areas. As a result urbanization increased to 36.8 percent by 1960.

Intermediate urbanization

Rapid urbanization took place between 1960 and 1990. From 35.8 percent in 1960, urbanization reached 82.6 percent by 1990, a 46.8 percentage point increase. Thus after 1960, urbanization increased an average 15.6 percent every 10 years. In this urbanization phase, about 60 percent of the urban population lived in large cities (populations of more than 1 million). And concentration of urban population in satellite cities around the capital grew. The proportion of urban population living in the capital region rose from 21 percent in 1960 to 43 percent in 1990.

Advanced urbanization

Urbanization reached a plateau in the late 1990s at about 90 percent. Between 1990 and 2000, it increased from 83 percent to 94 percent, and remained almost unchanged at 96 percent as of 2005. Concentration of the urban population in the capital region continued (48 percent in 2005). Some residents living in the core of metropolitan cities started to relocate to neighboring cities and satellite towns with populations between 200,000 and 1 million.

The evolution of urbanization policies in Korea

Korea's progress from incipient to advanced urbanization involved four policy areas: urban planning and land management, housing supply policies, connecting policies, and slum and low-income housing policies.

Before the introduction of a comprehensive urban planning system, land development programs were established, followed by a land use regulation system. Korea suffered greatly from its housing shortage, with no apparent housing polices during the incipient and intermediate urbanization periods. Housing shortages were solved to some extent by the massive housing construction plans in the early 1990s.

The transportation system was completed in the following order: first, the railroad system at the incipient stage, followed by the express highway system in the intermediate urbanization period, and then the metropolitan highway and high speed railroad system in the advanced period.

In the intermediate period, policies that cleared and relocated slums were implemented in response to spatial division in urban areas, but with no success. In the early advanced period, the decline of slums was driven mainly by the strong market forces in the residential redevelopment projects.

Throughout the urbanization process, urban planning and land management have been considered the most important policy areas.

Urban planning and land management

In the incipient urbanization stage, modern land ownership and land management institutions were established. The Land Survey Act (1912) and the Urban Planning Act (1934) defined the rights of land ownership and land use.

Established in 1962, the Land Acquisition Act provided an institutional means for appropriate compensation in purchasing land. Public works projects greatly increased during this period, and the Exemption Act for Public Land Acquisition and Compensation was introduced in 1975 to facilitate public land acquisition with proper compensation. It provided uniform evaluation criteria, methods, and processes to acquire lands for public works.

Residential development projects for the sale and rent of affordable housing were first adopted through the Public Housing Act in 1963, but land development was still carried out through land readjustment projects. In 1966, the Korean government established the Land Readjustment Act and separated it from the existing Urban Planning Act. The Urban Redevelopment Act was newly established and separated from the Urban Planning Act in 1971. In 1973, the government instituted the Promotion Act of Industrial Base Development to develop industrial sites and promote industrialization. The act provided a legal basis to purchase lands within the area designated as industrial districts, including compulsory acquisition.

During this intermediate stage of urbanization, several complementary measures were required for a number of reasons. For instance, zoning decisions and urban planning facility projects were amended too frequently by the mayors and county leaders. To solve this problem, the Urban Comprehensive Plan—which provides guidelines for 20-year urban planning visions, zoning decisions, and urban planning facilities—became mandatory. And downtown development projects were implemented according to phased development scenarios in the Urban Comprehensive Plan.

As urbanization was under way at full speed, urban development projects greatly increased, and goals, subjects, and types of development projects became diverse. But too many acts and measures were established, leading to confusion within the urban development system. In the late 1990s, a movement to integrate and reorganize urban planning acts emerged. For example, the National Land Use and Management Act, established in 2002, integrated the Urban Planning Act and the National Land Use Management Act, which had separately controlled urban and nonurban areas. It played a major role in spreading urban planning throughout the country.

In the 1990s, the number of registered vehicles greatly increased, and transportation infrastructure rapidly expanded. Cooperation between the city and the national government was emphasized to accommodate urban infrastructure. As a response to these regional planning issues, metropolitan city–regional planning, which requires cooperation between the city and the county or the city and the province, was institutionalized in 2000.

Housing supply policies

Although providing sufficient housing units in response to rapid urban population growth is necessary to meet basic infrastructure needs, housing supply policies were not a major concern during the incipient urbanization stage.

In the intermediate urbanization stage, however, housing shortages became serious social issues and gradually worsened due to rapid urban growth.

Recognizing this problem, the government built a large number of housing units. Because of the scarcity of urban land and high population density, it encouraged the construction of apartments rather than houses. Its housing construction policies, such as the Housing Construction Promotion Act (1973) and the Two Million Housing Construction Plan (1988–92), led to large-scale residential development focused on apartment construction. Due to these policy efforts, the most serious housing problems were largely solved in the advanced urbanization stage.

Connecting policies

Because the Kyoungbu (Seoul-Busan) railroad was built in 1904, and a railroad network had already been established in the early Japanese colonial period, Korea was prepared for a more modern urban structure in the incipient urbanization stage. In the intermediate urbanization stage, road networks based on expressways were built, contributing to the development of nationwide transportation systems. In the latter half of the intermediate urbanization stage, urban highways and subway lines were built to meet rapidly rising demand in large metropolitan areas. In the advanced urbanization stage, the Korea Train Express (KTX, the bullet train) was constructed, shrinking the entire nation into a half-day travel zone. In the 2000s, regional highways such as the Seoul Outer Beltway were constructed in major metropolitan cities to meet metro-regional transport demand.

The government considered trunk transport infrastructure a core component of the national economic development planning. The first Five-Year Economic Development Plan (1962–66) devoted 64 percent of the total investment in transportation to railroads. The second Five-Year Plan focused on metropolitan roads and a "public road–centric" structure. The third to fifth Five-Year Plans focused on expanding expressway capacities. The sixth (1987–91) emphasized pavement projects, increasing the pavement ratio from 54 to 76 percent.

Slums and low-income housing policies

In the incipient urbanization stage, land ownership by a few landlords or the ruling class forced farmers to lose their land and move to urban areas. In the intermediate stage, industrialization provided incentives for rural people to move to cities for job opportunities. While this concentration of rural population in urban areas was in progress, many deteriorated low-income neighborhoods (slums)—such as shanty towns and poor hillside settlements—formed within urban areas.

Later in the intermediate urbanization stage, these neighborhoods were removed for more efficient land use, and many apartments replaced these poor-quality houses. Dense slums were greatly reduced in the advanced urbanization stage. But the residents from these slums were scattered over outer metropolitan areas or satellite cities, living in substandard places such as in building attics or basements.

Looking ahead

Urban planning and land management institutions were adopted to respond to challenges in each urbanization stage and proved their effectiveness. Investments in connective infrastructure contributed to the successful urbanization process by improving the economic efficiency of the national urban system as well as that of individual cities. Construction of the KTE line helped reduce travel time dramatically, forming a spatial structure suitable for the advanced urbanization stage.

But the absence of housing supply policies from incipient to intermediate urbanization stages continuously raised housing and land prices. As a solution, increased housing supply, through direct and indirect government interventions, helped stabilize housing prices, but demand for high-quality residential environments still poses heavy financial burdens on the national and household economy.

VIETNAM

Vietnam will have only one chance to get urbanization right. If we fail at urbanization, we will fail at industrialization and modernization.
—Deputy P. M. Nguyen Sinh Hung, speaking at the Vietnam National Urban Conference, November 6–7, 2009

Vietnam is now widely considered a developmental success story. Driven by the *Doi Moi* reforms that began in 1986, Vietnam has rapidly evolved from one of the poorest countries in the world to an emerging middle-income country. In about 25 years, living standards have tripled, poverty has fallen by 80 percent, and gross national income per capita has risen from less than $100 to more than $1,000. With its accession to the World Trade Organization in 2007, Vietnam emerged as a global and regional powerhouse: international trade represents 160 percent of GDP, exports have risen by 14 percent annually over 2006–10, and many industrial exports have grown much faster. As of 2011, Vietnam attracted more net foreign direct investment commitments than Indonesia, the Philippines, and Thailand combined (World Bank 2011b).

The country's long-term development prospects are solid, but the sustainability of its growth will necessitate a shift from reliance on low-cost labor and natural resources exploitation to a greater focus on productivity growth and technological advances while also ensuring greater macroeconomic stability (World Bank 2011a). Urbanization

is a central element of Vietnam's economic growth strategy. No country has achieved high-income status and strong economic growth without urbanizing, and nearly all countries become at least 50 percent urbanized before reaching middle-income status. Vietnam is on this path. Urbanization will be rapid for the next 10–15 years, and 50 percent of the country's population will be living in urban areas by 2025.

How Vietnam is urbanizing

Vietnam has a complex system for classifying cities, including two cities with *Special* status due to their significant and unique economic and political contributions to the country: Ho Chi Minh City and Hanoi. Then cities are classified from Class I to Class V in descending order of size, with Class V marking the limit between rural and urban areas.[1] Besides these two, Vietnam has at least two others with populations of more than 1 million (Can Tho and Hai Phong) and several medium cities (such as Da Nang, with a population of about 700,000). But most of Vietnam's economic and population growth is driven by two independent, dominant, core-periphery urban systems: Ho Chi Minh City and Hanoi (map 4.3).

At this stage of Vietnam's development, as gains from agglomeration economies are consolidated, the dominance of the major economic regions of the southeast (Ho Chi Minh City) and the Red River Delta (Hanoi), together with the emerging Mekong Delta economic region, are to be expected. But these regions appear to be developing in different ways, with some evidence that Hanoi is moving more rapidly into heavy and higher technology manufacturing, while Ho Chi Minh City and the southeast region still dominate economic and manufacturing output (map 4.4).

Vietnam's economic growth and competitiveness will depend largely on these regions, and sustaining strategic investments in these areas is important for economic development. Notwithstanding the rise of urban economic centers, rural areas are still the

The World Bank's Vietnam Urbanization Review was led by Dean Cira, and prepared by a core team consisting of Arish Dastur, Henry Jewell, Austin Kilroy, Nancy Lozano-Garcia, Huyen Thi Phuong Phan, and Hyoung Gun Wang. The team benefited from the strategic guidance provided by Stephen Karam and Somik V. Lall. The consultants and firms that helped prepare background reports for this work are Alain Bertaud, Etude Economique Conseil, Quang Minh Consulting, Mekong Economics, and Urban Solutions. The Vietnam Urbanization Review was informed and enriched by extensive and valuable discussions with the government of Vietnam.

MAP 4.3   Population and GDP are highly concentrated

a. Population   b. GDP per capita

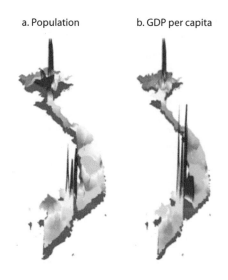

Source: Authors' calculations, based on data from the Vietnam General Statistics Office.

MAP 4.4   Ho Chi Minh City dominates economic and manufacturing output

a. Total economic output   b. Manufacturing output

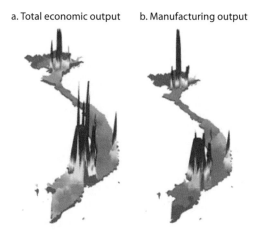

Source: Authors' calculation, based on data from the Vietnam General Statistics Office.

major source of livelihood for a large part of Vietnam's population and 93 percent of its poor. For areas currently without strong economic potential comparable with large cities, investing in people (education and health),

infrastructure, and universal access to basic services will level the playing field and facilitate the fluidity of factor markets, enabling firms and households to choose the best locations for economic activity, thus maximizing Vietnam's economic development.

Urban challenges

Valuing and pricing urban land
Land markets in Vietnam reflect deeper issues with land management and governance. Vietnamese cities have largely enabled a pluralistic supply of housing to meet the needs of different market segments—through small contractors producing town houses, incremental upgrading of housing stock, and infrastructure extension to increase the density of peri-urban areas. But land prices are by most indications high, partly due to Vietnam's two-tiered land pricing system and a lack of good market information. In Hanoi and Ho Chi Minh City, land and housing prices produced by formal developers are perhaps affordable to only 5 percent of the population.

Planning
Planning and urban management in Vietnam still focus on static urban design principles—not on the fluid functioning of land and housing markets. Strict adherence to static Master Plans, combined with a city classification system that induces cities to annex rural areas and land lease for infrastructure financing, are leading to urban sprawl and new towns where there is little market demand (map 4.5).

Basic urban services
Vietnam has done a remarkable job attaining nearly universal access to electricity (96 percent). Access to other basic services such as water and sanitation remains at lower levels despite remarkable improvement (70 percent of urban households had access to piped water by 2007). In contrast, waste water collection and treatment levels are still very low. And it appears that access to and quality of urban services diminishes with city size.

MAP 4.5   Hanoi's Master Plan for new towns contrasted with the plan of a compact city (Seoul)

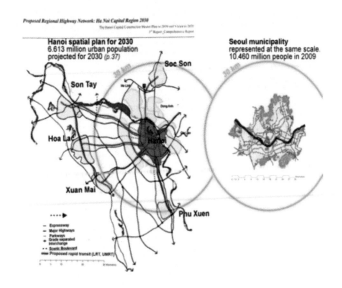

Source: Bertaud 2011.

As Vietnam moves to higher income levels and as universal access is achieved in other services, the next goal will be to focus on the quality and sustainability of urban services. Tariffs for urban water supply generally cover only operations and maintenance costs, and nonrevenue water (losses) is as high as 40 percent in major cities. A major challenge for local governments will be financing infrastructure services. As service quality improves, tariffs will need to rise to cover investment costs as well (to the extent possible). Local governments have limited options to raise own-source revenues for investment and rely increasingly on land sales (leases); for example, such sales made up 20 percent of Ho Chi Minh City's 2008 budget. Continuing strong investment in cities will depend on more sustainable financing.

Connections among neighborhoods within cities

Vietnam's cities (including its largest) have relatively good mobility, due in part to the predominant use of motorcycles. But this is changing rapidly. As incomes rise, so will

car ownership. As motorists shift to individual cars for just a fraction of the current trips made by motorcycles, the current road networks in Hanoi and Ho Chi Minh City (to a slightly less extent) will be incompatible with the demand for road space. A priority will be road networks and transit systems that are compatible with rising urban densities and land use trends (such as the emerging policy-centric development of the major cities) and that reflect consumer demand for location of housing and commercial facilities. This will require integrating land use planning and development with transit and urban transport development. Minimizing the transition from motorbike to car while Vietnam's major cities develop their transit networks will be a major challenge, yet it is a priority to ensure greater mobility in Vietnam's cities.

Connections between metropolitan cores and peripheries

The connectivity of the urban system underscores the importance of investing in regional economic growth drivers. Ho Chi Minh City and the southeast together with the Mekong Delta Region account for 62 percent of Vietnam's industrial activity, and Ho Chi Minh City and the southeast Region account for 71 percent of the country's seaport throughput. From 1999–2009, the bulk of manufacturing employment and its highest growth were in Hanoi and Ho Chi Minh City and their neighboring suburban areas (within 70 kilometers from the city center). Even at this early stage of urbanization, manufacturing activities are not confined to the administrative boundaries and, in many cases, there is strong manufacturing activity within a 50-kilometer radius of the two major cities. Investing in logistics infrastructure will be critical to developing the country's strongest economic regions. An intercity trucking survey conducted for the Urbanization Review indicates that transport costs are highest in the two main economic regions. Truckers identify poor road conditions and informal payments as the major bottlenecks. This suggests that connections can be improved not only through strategic transport and logistics improvements, but also through regulatory reforms to improve service quality in trucking and logistics services. Analysis suggests that freight costs in the Ho Chi Minh City and Hanoi economic regions could be reduced 57 percent and 67 percent, respectively, by reducing these bottlenecks.

Financing

Provinces and their subsidiary units are financing themselves through a range of sources: equalization transfers from the central government, taxes, land sales, short-term debt, local development investment funds, and sometimes cross-subsidies from profitable subsidiary entities of provincial public utility companies. The merits and risks of these approaches need to be further examined as alternatives are considered. For the poorer provinces, equalization has been a cornerstone in enabling access to basic services and should be maintained.

Looking ahead

Planning

Monitoring land and housing markets will be important to help urban economies function efficiently and equitably. Moving from static to dynamic plans, better integrating planning functions, and using sharper tools to monitor real changes in land and housing markets could improve the planning process considerably and lead to a more efficient allocation of land uses.

Connecting

To ensure that transit systems are compatible with urban density and land use trends, it will be necessary to coordinate land use planning and development with transit and urban transport development. Minimizing the transition from motorbike to car while Vietnam's major cities develop their transit networks will be a major challenge and priority to ensure greater mobility in Vietnam's cities.

Connections can be improved not only through strategic transport and logistics improvements, but also through regulatory reforms to improve service quality in trucking and logistics services.

Financing

Because local governments have limited options to raise own-source revenues for investment, sustaining strong investment in cities will depend on more sustainable sources of financing.

Note

1. Classification is not only based on population. It also takes into account density, percentages of nonagricultural labor, and socioeconomic infrastructure available.

References

Bertaud, Alain. 2011. "Comments on Hanoi Capital Construction Master Plan to 2030 and Vision to 2050 (3rd report—comprehensive text report)." Commissioned for Vietnam Urbanization Review, World Bank, Washington, DC.

World Bank. 2011a. "Country Partnership Strategy for Vietnam." Working Draft, World Bank, Washington, DC. September 9.

———. 2011b. *Securing the Present, Shaping the Future.* East Asia and Pacific Economic Update 2011, Volume 1. Washington, DC: World Bank.